# LETTERS

ON

# THE STATE OF CHRISTIANITY

IN

# INDIA

# LETTERS

ON

# THE STATE OF CHRISTIANITY

IN

# INDIA,

IN WHICH

## THE CONVERSION OF THE HINDOOS

IS CONSIDERED AS IMPRACTICABLE,

ABBE J.A. DUBOIS

GYAN

*Published by*

Gyan Publishing House
5, Ansari Road
Daryaganj, New Delhi-110002
Phone: 011-47034999, 9811692060
E-mail: books@gyanbooks.com

*Distribution Network*
gyanbooks.com
India, USA, Canada, UK, Australia



ISBN: 978-93-7014-726-3 (HB)

First Published, 1823

2nd Impression 2025

*Printed at:* Gyan Press, Delhi.



**LETTERS ON THE STATE OF CHRISTIANITY IN INDIA**
Author: ABBE J.A. DUBOIS

# LETTERS

ON

# THE STATE OF CHRISTIANITY

IN

# INDIA;

IN WHICH

THE CONVERSION OF THE HINDOOS

IS CONSIDERED AS IMPRACTICABLE.

TO WHICH IS ADDED,

## *A VINDICATION OF THE HINDOOS,*

MALE AND FEMALE,

IN ANSWER TO A SEVERE ATTACK MADE UPON BOTH BY

THE REVEREND *****.

---

BY THE ABBÉ J. A. DUBOIS,

MISSIONARY IN MYSORE,

AUTHOR OF THE DESCRIPTION OF THE PEOPLE OF INDIA.

---

Cujus vult miseretur, et quem vult indurat. ROM. ix. 18.

---

LONDON:

PRINTED FOR

LONGMAN, HURST, REES, ORME, BROWN, AND GREEN,

PATERNOSTER-ROW.

1823.

TO

THE HONOURABLE

# THE COURT OF DIRECTORS,

AS A MARK OF HIS GRATITUDE,

AND AS A TESTIMONY OF HIS MOST SINCERE WISHES

FOR THE TEMPORAL WELFARE OF THEIR

*HINDOO SUBJECTS*,

AFTER HAVING VAINLY ENDEAVOURED TO PROMOTE

THEIR SPIRITUAL INTERESTS,

DURING A LONG RESIDENCE OF THIRTY-TWO YEARS

AMONG THEM, AS A RELIGIOUS TEACHER,

THESE LETTERS

ARE MOST RESPECTFULLY INSCRIBED

BY

THEIR MOST OBEDIENT

AND FAITHFUL SERVANT,

THE AUTHOR.

# ADVERTISEMENT.

These Letters were written at several periods, to friends who had asked the Author's opinion on the subjects therein discussed. Two of them, the second and third, were addressed to a dignitary of the established church, a learned and liberal-minded gentleman, who, so far from taking offence at the candour and freedom with which the Author expresses his sentiments, was pleased to return him his unqualified thanks for the same. The others were addressed to friends, who appeared equally satisfied at the independent, candid, and impartial manner in which the subject was treated, and who encouraged him to have the whole published for the information of the Public, among whom much misapprehension prevailed, chiefly occasioned by many erroneous statements, published of late years at home, by many well-intentioned authors, who, misled by too warm a zeal, and mistaking their own religious creed as the common standard which should rule all the human race, and knowing nothing, or very little of the invincible attachment of the people of India to their religion and customs, expected to be able to overcome the insurmountable religious prejudices of the Hindoos, and bring them at once to their own faith.

The Author has endeavoured to state (as well as his very imperfect acquaintance with the English language has enabled him to do) with freedom, candour, and simplicity, the desperateness of such an attempt. His notions on the subject are derived from an experience of thirty-two years of confidential and quite unrestrained intercourse among the natives of India, of all castes, religions, and ranks; during which, in order to win their confidence, and remove suspicion, as far as possible, he has constantly lived like them, embracing their manners, customs, and most of their prejudices, in his dress, his diet, their rules of civility, and good-breeding, and their mode of intercourse in the world. But the restraints under which he has lived during so long a period of his life, have proved of no advantage to him in promoting the sacred cause in which he was engaged as a religious teacher. During that time he has vainly, in his exertions to promote the cause of Christianity, watered the soil of India with his sweats, and many times with his tears, at the sight of the quite insurmountable obduracy of the people he had to deal with; ready to water it with his blood, if his doing so had been able to overcome the invincible resistance he had to encounter every where, in his endeavours to disseminate some gleams of the evangelical light. Every where the seeds sown by him have fallen upon a naked rock, and have instantly dried away.

At length, entirely disgusted at the total inutility of his pursuits, and warned by his grey hair that it was full time to think of his own concerns, he has returned to Europe, to pass in retirement the few days he may still have to live, and get ready to give in his accounts to his Redeemer.

These Letters are now brought without pretensions before the public, whose indulgence the Author solicits, chiefly in what may appear deficient in point of style. What he states is not from hearsay, it is the result of a long and attentive experience; and he will feel himself sufficiently rewarded for his troubles, if his candid and unaffected statements can prove of any utility to a liberal and indulgent Public.

LONDON, *June* 19. 1823.

# LETTER I.

To W. J. Esq.—*Mysore.*

My dear Sir,

Some time ago, when conversing with you on the subject of proselytism in India, which seems of late to have considerably attracted the attention of the public in England, and to have given rise to much discussion among enlightened persons, you appeared astonished at the freedom of my opinions; and in order to justify them, I promised you a further statement of my sentiments in writing. I will now endeavour to fulfil my engagements, if not with ability at least with fairness and candour.

The question to be considered may be reduced to these two points: First, Is there a possibility of making real converts to Christianity among the natives in India? Secondly, Are the means employed for that purpose, and above all, the translation of the Holy Scriptures into the idioms of the country, likely to conduce to this desirable object?

To both interrogatories I will answer in the negative: it is my decided opinion, first, that under existing circumstances there is no human possibility of converting the Hindoos, to any sect of christianity, and, secondly, that the translation of the Holy Scriptures circulated among them, so far from conducing to this end, will, on the contrary, increase the prejudices of the natives against the christian religion, and prove in many respects detrimental to it. These assertions, coming from a person of my profession, may to many appear bold and extraordinary; I will therefore support them by such arguments and proofs as a long experience and practice in the career of proselytism have enabled me to adduce.

Before I go farther, it will not be amiss to say a few words about the manner in which the christian religion was first brought into the country; and on the industry with which its interests were managed by the first preachers.

The christian religion of the catholic persuasion was introduced into India a little more than three hundred years ago; at the epoch of the Portuguese invasions. One of the first missionaries was the famous St. Francis Xavier, a Spanish jesuit of the greatest merit, and animated with a truly apostolical zeal, and still known under the appellation of the *Apostle of India.* He traversed several provinces of India, and is said to have made many thousand converts, at a period when the prejudices of the natives against the christian religion were far from reaching the height they have since attained. The cast of fishermen at Cape Comorin, who are all christians, still pride themselves in being the offspring of the first proselytes made by that apostle.

Xavier soon discovered in the manners and prejudices of the natives an insurmountable bar to the progress of christianity among them, as appears from the printed letters still extant, which he wrote to St. Ignatius de Loyola, his superior, and the founder of the order of the jesuits.

At last Francis Xavier, entirely disheartened by the invincible obstacles he every where met in his apostolic career, and by the apparent impossibility of making real converts, left the country in disgust, after a stay in it of only two or three years; and he embarked for Japan, where his spiritual labours were crowned with far greater success, and laid the foundation of those once numerous and flourishing congregations of Japanese christians, who, within a period of less than a century, amounted to more than a million of souls. At this time their daily-increasing numbers threatening to supplant the religion of the country, awakened the jealousy and alarm of the Bonzes and other directors of the popular faith, and gave rise to one of the severest persecutions ever recorded in the annals of christianity, and which ended in the total extermination of the christians. After an interval of nearly two hundred years, this spirit of intolerance and persecution is still continued, as appears from the conduct observed to this day by the Japanese government towards the Europeans trading to their shores, and from some other circumstances.

The disappointment and want of success of Xavier ought to have been sufficient to damp the most fervent zeal of the persons disposed to enter the same career. When a man of his temper, talents, and virtues, had been baffled in all his endeavours to introduce christianity into India, his successors could scarcely flatter themselves with the hope of being more fortunate. However, this was not the case. His jesuit brethren in Europe were not to be deterred by difficulties or contradictions in undertaking, where the cause of religion was at stake. In consequence, jesuits were sent from every catholic country to India, to forward the interests of the gospel.

By degrees those missionaries introduced themselves into the inland country. They saw that in order to fix the attention of these people, gain their confidence, and get a hearing, it was indispensably necessary to respect their prejudices, and even to conform to their dress, their manner of living, and forms of society; in short, scrupulously to adopt the costumes and practices of the country.

With this persuasion, they at their first outset announced themselves as European Brahmins come from a distance of five thousand leagues from the western parts of the *Djamboody*, for the double purpose of imparting and receiving knowledge from their brother Brahmins in India. Almost all these first missionaries were more or less acquainted with astronomy or medicine; the two sciences best calculated to ingratiate them with the natives of every description.

After announcing themselves as Brahmins, they made it their study to imitate that tribe: they put on a Hindoo dress of cavy, or yellow colour, the same as that used by the Indian religious teachers and penitents; they made frequent ablutions; whenever they showed themselves in public they applied to their foreheadpaste, made of sandal wood, as used by the Brahmins. They scrupulously abstained from every kind of animal food, as well as from intoxicating liquors, entirely faring like Brahmins on vegetables and milk; in a word, after the example of St. Paul (1 *Cor.* ix. 20. 21.) "Unto the Jews, they became as Jews, that they might gain the Jews; to them that were without law, as without law. They were made all things to all men, that they might by all means save some." It was by such a life of almost incredible privations and restraints, that they insinuated themselves among these people.

Fully aware of the unalterable attachment of the natives to their own usages and practices, they made it their principal study not to hurt their feelings, by attacking all at once the superstitions with which most of their customs are infested: they judged it more prudent at the beginning to overlook many of them, and wait for a more favourable time, to put the converts right on the subject. Their colour, their talents, their virtues, above all, their perfect disinterestedness, rendered them acceptable even to the Hindoo princes, who, astonished at the novelty and singularity of the circumstance, bestowed their protection on these extraordinary men, and gave them full freedom to preach their religion, and make proselytes to it.

The jesuits began their work under these favourable auspices, and made a great number of converts among all castes of Hindoos, in those countries where they were allowed the free exercise of their religious functions. It appears from authentic lists, made up about seventy years ago, which I have seen, that the number of native christians in these countries was as follows, viz. in the Marawa about 30,000, in the Madura above 100,000, in the Carnatic 80,000, in Mysore 35,000. At the present time hardly a third of this number is to be found in these districts respectively. I have heard that the number of converts was still much more considerable on the other coast, from Goa to Cape Comorin; but of these I never saw authentic lists.

Things were carrying on in this promising manner by the Jesuit missionaries, when severe complaints were preferred against them from several parts to the Holy See at Rome. The accusers were chiefly friars of other religious orders, settled at Goa and Pondicherry, who accused the Jesuits of the most culpable indulgence, in tolerating and winking at all kinds of idolatrous superstitions among their proselytes, and with having themselves rather become converts to the idolatrous worship of the Hindoo, by conforming to many of their practices and superstitions, than making Indians converts to the christian religion.

The charges had some degree of foundation, though not to the extent set forth by the accusers, whose representations seem on the whole to have proceeded rather from motives of envy and jealousy against the jesuits, than from a true disinterested zeal for the cause of religion.

Those often-repeated accusations gave rise to a long and warm correspondence between the parties concerned, in which the jesuits, in giving an account of their conduct to the Holy See, did not conceal that, from motives of prudence, and not to risk the revolt of the converts, and prejudice the pagans more and more against the new religion, they had been under the very unpleasant necessity of overlooking many reprehensible practices, waiting for fitter circumstances to suppress them gradually. At the same time they exposed the dangers which could not fail to ensue, if the feelings of the Hindoos were all at once hurt on this extremely delicate point, and the practices justly complained of, openly opposed and reprobated, before the christian religion had gained a solid footing in the country.

They endeavoured to give weight to their assertions, and excuse their conduct, by the example of the apostles themselves, who at the beginning of their apostolic career judged it prudent from regard to the prejudices of the Jews, and in order to encourage their conversion, to tolerate *circumcision* among them, as well as their abstaining from blood, and from strangled things, and the observance of many other judaical customs.

All these and many other like reasons appeared to the Holy See futile and merely evasive; and the jesuits were peremptorily ordered to preach the catholic religion in all its purity, and altogether suppress the superstitious practices, till then tolerated among the Neophites.

The jesuits, seeing that their following such directions would not only put a stop to all further conversions, but also occasion the apostacy of a great many proselytes, before they gave up their point, sent deputations to Rome, in order to enlighten the Holy See on the subject. This disgusting contest, which was carried on in several instances with much acrimony, lasted more than forty years before it came to an end.

At length the reigning Pope, wishing to finish the business, sent Cardinal de Tournon to India with the title of apostolic legate, to make personal enquiries on the subject, and report all the details to the Holy See. The cardinal landed at Pondicherry about a century ago, and on his arrival sent for some of the principal missionaries, living in the inland country, had all matters minutely investigated, and made his report to the Pope. After some further delay, the famous and very learned Benedict XIV., having been raised to the papal chair, and wishing to put at once a stop to this scandalous contest, issued a very rigorous bull or decree in several articles, by which he formally and expressly condemned and reprobated all the superstitious practices (a list of which was contained in the instrument), till then tolerated by the missionaries, and required that the whole of them, of whatever order or dignity they might be, should bind themselves by a solemn oath taken before a bishop, to conform themselves without any tergiversation whatever to the spirit and letter of the decree; it was moreover ordered, that the decree should be read and published every Sunday in all churches and chapels in the presence of the congregation, and a promise of submission to it be required from all converts.

These orders were reluctantly complied

with: but what the jesuits had foreseen happened:—a great number of proselytes preferred renouncing the new religion to abandoning their practices. A stop was put to conversions; and the christian religion began to become odious to the Hindoos on account of its intolerance.

At that very time happened the European invasion, and the bloody contests for dominion between the English and French. The Europeans, till then almost entirely unknown to the natives in the interior, introduced themselves in several ways and under various denominations into every part of the country. The Hindoos soon found that those missionaries, whom their colour, their talents, and other qualities, had induced them to regard as such extraordinary beings, as men coming from another world, were in fact nothing else but disguised *Fringy* (Europeans); * and that their country, their religion, and original education, were the same with those of the vile, the contemptible Fringy, who had of late invaded their country. This event proved the last blow to the interests of the christian religion. No more conversions were made;

* *Fringy*, is the appellation under which the Europeans are designated by the natives of India; it is derived from the term Frank, and has been introduced by the Mahometans.

apostacy became almost general in several quarters; and christianity became more and more an object of contempt and aversion, in proportion as the European manners became better known to the Hindoos.

Nearly at that period the suppression of the order of the jesuits took place in Europe; and there being no longer a sufficient number of missionaries, a national black clergy was formed, and the attendance on the remaining congregations entrusted to their care. Those native missionaries not having the advantage of a proper education, and many amongst them shewing themselves more attached to their own interests than to those of religion, enjoy but little consideration even among their flocks, and none among the natives of any other description.

Such is the abridged history of the rise, the progress, and the decline of the christian religion in India. The low state to which it is now reduced, and the contempt in which it is held, cannot be surpassed. There is not at present in the country (as mentioned before) more than a third of the christians who were to be found in it eighty years ago, and this number diminishes every day by frequent apostacy. It will dwindle to nothing in a short period; and if things continue as they are now going on, within less than fifty years there will, I fear, remain no vestige of christianity among the natives.

The christian religion, which was formerly an object of indifference, or at most of contempt, is at present become, I will venture to say, almost an object of horror. It is certain that during the last sixty years no proselytes or but a very few have been made. Those christians who are still to be met with in several parts of the country, and whose numbers (as I have just mentioned,) diminishes every day, are the offspring of the converts made by the jesuits before that period. The very small number of proselytes who are still gained over from time to time, are found among the lowest tribes; so are individuals who, driven out from their castes, on account of their vices or scandalous transgressions of their usages, are shunned afterwards by every body as outlawed men, and have no other resource left than that of turning christians, in order to form new connexions in society; and you will easily fancy that such an assemblage of the offals and dregs of society only tends to increase the contempt and aversion entertained by the Hindoos against christianity.

In fact, how can our holy religion prosper amidst so many insurmountable obstacles? A person who embraces it becomes a proscribed and outlawed man; he loses at once all that can attach him to life. A husband, a father is forthwith forsaken and deserted by his own wife and children, who obstinately refuse to have any further intercourse with their degraded relative. A son is unmercifully driven out of his paternal mansion, and entirely deserted by those who gave him birth.

By embracing the christian religion, therefore, a Hindoo loses his all. Relations, kindred, friends,—all desert him! Goods, possessions, inheritance, all disappear!

Where is the man furnished with a sufficient stock of cynical fortitude to be able to bear such severe trials?

The very name of christian carries along with it the stain of infamy; and the proposal alone to become a convert to christianity is considered by every well-bred Hindoo as a very serious insult, which is instantly resented, as I have witnessed in repeated instances. Such a proposal must always be made with the greatest prudence and circumspection, in order not to be exposed to severe reproof from those to whom it is addressed.

Fully aware of the dispositions of the Hindoos in this respect, and that forced religious controversies with them can answer no good purpose, and generally produces but bad effects, I have always made it my rule, in the visits I from time to time receive from pagans of every caste, when visiting my several congregations, never to obtrude myself upon them on religious subjects, unless urged by them, which is often the case; a great many among them being fond of discoursing upon religion; some from motives of curiosity, but a greater number from vanity, and to have an opportunity of making a display of their pretended learning, as well as of becoming acquainted with the learning and mental resources of their opponents.

When attacked on this subject, the necessity of standing on the defensive obliges me to enter into discussions, and set forth the excellence of the christian religion, over the absurdities of paganism; employing for this purpose such short, plain, and simple reasoning, as may be within the comprehension of my hearers; for deep and learned arguments could not be understood by them.

On such occasions, when the arguments of my opponents in vindication of their own religion are exhausted, and they have nothing more to say, they rarely fail to conclude and sum up their reasoning by this solemn and, in their mind, unanswerable appeal, exclaiming with much exultation and emphasis, "After all, your religion is the religion of the *Fringy;*" refraining, however, from a feeling of respect, or perhaps from motives of prudence, from adding, in my presence, the second part of this forcible sentence, viz. " and all that comes from so impure a source must be radically bad."

In the mean time, when compelled to sustain religious disputes with pagans, I am far from imitating the forbidding and provoking conduct of some uncivil and intolerant persons of my profession, who, instigated by a warm, a false, and in many instances a perilous zeal, on their first outset, when disputing upon religion with the heathen, begin their arguments with these opprobrious and insulting phrases, " All your gods are nothing else but demons; you all will go to hell to expiate in eternal flames the crime of your idolatry;" and such like vituperative language. Such a strain of abuse and insult only tends, as may be expected, to provoke a return of blasphemous expressions against the christian religion and its divine author; and to render christianity itself, its teachers, and its followers, more and more odious to the natives.

In my religious controversy I never forget the decorum, calmness, forbearance, and mutual regard that ought ever to be observed in such circumstances, carefully avoiding all that could to no good purpose wound the feelings and prejudices of my opponents; and if I reap no other fruit from my trouble, but their reluctant assent to my simple arguments, I can at least pride myself, that on such occasions I get a patient and cheerful hearing, and that both my opponents and myself separate on good terms, satisfied with the mutual respect with which the dispute was carried on. But to return.

The christian religion is at the present time become so odious, that in several parts of the country a Hindoo, who should happen to have friends or connexions among the natives professing this religion, would not dare to own it in public, as he would be exposed to severe reproof for holding a familiar intercourse with (in their opinion) people so degraded.

Such is the state of degradation to which christianity has been reduced in these latter times, and which must be imputed in a great degree to the immoral and irregular conduct of many Europeans in every part of the country.

Besides the christians of the catholic persuasion, there are still existing in some parts of the country small congregations of the Lutheran sect; but they are held, if possible, in a still higher degree of contempt than the former.

The Lutheran mission was established at

*Tranqubar* a little more than a century ago. There were at all times among the missionaries of this sect respectable persons, distinguished by their talents and virtues; but they had only trifling successes in the work of proselytism: it could not be otherwise; the protestant religion being too simple in its worship to attract the attention of the Hindoo: as it has no show, no pomp, no outward ceremonies capable of making a strong impression on the senses, it was of course disliked by a quite sensual people, and has never had any considerable success.

If any of the several modes of christian worship were calculated to make an impression and gain ground in the country, it is no doubt the catholic form which you protestants call an idolatry in disguise: it has a *Pooga* or sacrifice; (the mass is termed by the Hindoos *Pooga*, literally, sacrifice;) it has processions, images, statues, *tirtan* or holy-water, fasts, *tittys* or feasts, and prayers for the dead, invocation of saints, &c., all which practices bear more or less resemblance to those in use among the Hindoos. Now, if even such a mode of worship is become so objectionable to the natives, can it be reasonably expected that any one of the simple protestant sects will ever prosper among them? The contrary has till now been the case. I have just observed that the Lutheran missionaries have had no sensible success during more than a century. At the present time their congregations are reduced to four or five: the most worthy of notice are, one at Vepery near Madras, consisting of about five or six hundred souls; another at Trankbar, composed of about twelve hundred; another at Tanjore, of nearly the same number; and a fourth at Trichinopoly, of about three or four hundred.

There are besides a few protestant christians dispersed chiefly in the Tinnivelly district, but in such small numbers that they do not deserve the name of congregations. When I was at Vellore, four years ago, in attendance on a numerous congregation living in that place, having been informed that the Lutheran missionaries kept a *catechist* or native religious teacher at that station, on a salary of five pagodas a month, I was led to suppose that they had a numerous flock there; but I was not a little surprised when, on enquiry, I found that the whole congregation consisted of only three individuals, namely, a drummer, a cook, and a horse-keeper.

In the meantime, do not suppose that those thin congregations are wholly composed of converted pagans; at least half consists of catholic apostates, who went over to the Lutheran sect in times of famine, or from other interested motives.

It is not uncommon on the coast to see natives who successively pass from one religion to another, according to their actual interest. In my last journey to Madras, I became acquainted with native converts who regularly changed their religion twice a year, and who for a long while were in the habit of being six months catholic, and six months protestant.

Besides the Lutheran sect, the Moravian brethren sent also missionaries to India, about seventy years ago, to make proselytes to their own persuasion. But on their first arrival in the country, they were so much amazed and appalled at the insurmountable difficulties to be met with every where, and so satisfied of the impossibility of making true converts to christianity among a people circumstanced as the Hindoos were, that very wisely they dropped their design without even making the attempt. They afterwards tried to convert the savage of the Nicobar Islands, but without success; at last, after lingering at Trankbar, where they had formed their principal establishment, during a period of nearly sixty years, and where I had the pleasure to pay them frequent visits when at that place in 1793, they were all recalled home about twenty years ago, and this sect no longer exists in India.

Respecting the new missionaries of several sects, who have of late years made their appearance in the country, you may rest assured, as far as my information on the subject goes, that notwithstanding the pompous reports made by several among them, all their endeavours to make converts have till now proved abortive, and that their successes are only to be seen on paper.

The sect of the Nestorians in Travancore is generally known: a short curious account of them is given by Gibbon in his history of the Roman empire; but a much fuller account was before written in French by La Croze, historiographer to the late Frederick King of Prussia, in a work in two small volumes, entitled *le Christianisme de l'Inde*. The late Dr. B. speaks of them; but I was surprised at the exaggerations of this learned author on this and many other important points. The fact is, that this sect, a colony of whom is supposed by some authors to have introduced itself into the Travancore country about the end of the eighth century, when Nestorianism was violently persecuted in Persia, once amounted to more than 100,000, (Gibbon says to 200,000 individuals). The jesuits, on their first arrival in India, hearing of them, in one way or another converted the greatest part to the catholic faith. Their liturgy is to this day in the Syrian language, and in the performance of their religious ceremonies they use this ancient dead tongue. There remains still among them large congregations, consisting of 70 or 80,000 christians, of whom two-thirds are catholics, and a third Nestorians. They are all designated under the contemptuous name of *Nazarany*, and held by the pagans in still greater contempt than the christians of this part of the country. The Nairs chiefly keep them at the greatest distance, and they form a separate body in society.

Both catholics and Nestorians have a native clergy of their own; and the clergy of both are equally ignorant, neither having the means of receiving a proper education. As their liturgy is in Syrian, all the science of their clergy consists in being able to read, or rather spell this language, in order to be qualified to perform their religious ceremonies. I have been assured, that there is at present no one amongst the catholic or the Nestorian clergy capable of properly understanding or explaining two phrases of the Syriac books. They have no houses of education, no teachers, no professors, but only some schools kept by their ignorant priests, for the purpose of teaching persons destined to the ecclesiastic profession, to read this language.

When the jesuits flourished in India, they took particular care to give a proper education to the persons of this class; and those who shewed a particular aptness for the sciences were sent to Rome for instruction, from whence they were sent back to their native country to be promoted to holy orders. Since the suppression of the jesuits, the Syrians being left to their own resources, it is not surprising that education among them has fallen into the low state in which it is now seen.

The catholic Syrians depend for their religious concerns upon the archbishop of Cronganor, and the Nestorians have a bishop of their own caste and sect.

I will conclude and sum up the first part of this account by repeating what I have already stated, that if any form of christianity were to make an impression and gain ground in the country, it is undoubtedly the catholic mode of worship, whose external pomp and shew appear so well suited to the genius and dispositions of the natives; and that when the catholic religion has failed to produce its effects, and its interests are become quite desperate, no other sect can flatter itself even with the remotest hopes of establishing its system: I trust that every unprejudiced and unbiassed mind will agree with me on this point.

I am in the meantime fully aware that a great many over-zealous protestants may be disposed to contradict this assertion, and maintain that the catholic religion being nothing but a corruption of the religion of Christ, and its worship a human invention, the divine assistance can never attend the propagation of it, and that its failure in the business of proselytism cannot be a matter of surprise.

Although a most sincere, and most undisguised Roman catholic, I am unwilling to enter here into a discussion foreign to my subject, on the respective merits or demerits either of the catholic or protestant persuasions. This is not the place to examine on what side are the innovations as well as corruptions of the word of God, so much complained of by both parties. I will even, for the sake of argument, suppose for an instant the catholic religion guilty of the superstitious innovations, abominations, and all kinds of idolatry laid to its charge by the other sects, and on this account unworthy of any claim to the divine assistance, in the propagation of its supposed corrupted tenets. But let us examine whether the other supposed more pure and unpolluted modes of christian worship have been more fortunate and successful in the work of proselytism in India.

Behold the Lutheran mission established in India more than a century ago! Interrogate its missionaries, ask them what were their successes during so long a period, and through what means were gained over the few proselytes they made? Ask them whether the interests of their sect are improving, or whether they are gaining ground, or whether their small numbers are not rather dwindling away?

Behold the truly industrious, the unaffected and unassuming Moravian brethren! Ask them how many converts they have made in India during a stay of about seventy years by preaching the gospel in all its naked simplicity? They will candidly answer, "Not one! not a single man!"

Behold the Nestorians in Travancore! Interrogate them; ask them for an account of their success in the work of proselytism in these modern times? Ask them whether they are gaining ground, and whether the interests of their ancient mode of worship is improving? They will reply, that so far from this being the case, their congregations once so flourishing, and amounting (according to Gibbon's account) to 200,000 souls, are now reduced to less than an eighth of this number, and are daily diminishing.

Behold the Baptist missionaries at Serampore! Inquire what are their spiritual successes on the shores of the Ganges? Ask them whether they have really the well-founded hope that their indefatigable labours in endeavouring to get the holy scriptures translated into all the idioms of India will increase their successes? Ask them whether those extremely incorrect versions, already obtained at an immense expense, have produced the sincere conversion of a single pagan? And I am persuaded, that if they are asked an answer upon their honour and conscience, they will all reply in the negative.

I will here conclude the first part of this account. What I have said of the state of the christian religion in India at the present and in former times, will, I trust, prove sufficient to make out what I have advanced, that there are in the actual circumstances of the case no human means to introduce christianity among the natives with any well-founded hopes of success.

I will now pass to the second division of my subject, viz. that should a possibility of further extending christianity exist, the means till now employed for this desirable end, and, above all, the translation of the holy scriptures into the several idioms of the country, circulated among the natives, will not only prove inadequate for the purpose, but also be injurious in many respects to the interests of the religion by increasing the prejudices of the natives against it. This assertion will perhaps appear bold, or even paradoxical to many persons who are but imperfectly acquainted with the prejudices of the Hindoos; I will therefore with simplicity and candour adduce the arguments on which my opinions are grounded.

You would perhaps look upon me as unqualified to give an unbiassed opinion on this topic, if in common with many misinformed protestants, you entertained the unfounded idea that the reading of the holy scriptures is forbidden to the catholics. This is one of the many calumnies spread against them, to render them odious to the other sects. So far from this being the case, the study of the holy writ is strongly recommended, and forms a leading feature of education in every seminary. What is required of the catholics on the subject is, that they shall not presume to interpret the text of the scriptures in a sense different from that of the church, or give it a meaning according to their own private judgment.

After having given you this explanation, I will resume my subject, and show that the naked text of the Bible, exhibited without a long previous preparation to the Hindoos, must prove detrimental to the christian religion, and increase their aversion to it, inasmuch as this sacred book contains in almost every page accounts which cannot fail deeply to wound their feelings, by openly hurting prejudices which are held most sacred.

To you who have some acquaintance with the education and customs of the Hindoos, I will put the following simple questions:

What will a well-bred native think, when, in reading over this holy book, he sees that Abraham, after receiving the visit of three angels under a human shape, entertains his guest by causing a calf to be killed, and served to them for their fare? The prejudiced Hindoo will at once judge that both Abraham and his heavenly guests were nothing but vile pariahs; and, without further reading, he will forthwith throw away the book, containing (in his opinions,) such sacrilegious accounts.

What will a Brahmin say, when he peruses the details of the bloody sacrifices prescribed in the mosaical law in the worship of the true God? He will assuredly declare, that the god who could be pleased with the shedding of the blood of so many victims immolated to his honour, must undoubtedly be a deity of the same kind (far be from me the blasphemy) as the mischievous Hindoo deities, Cohly, Mahry, Darma-rajah, and other infernal gods, whose wrath cannot be appeased but by the shedding of blood, and the immolating of living victims.

But, above all, what will a Brahmin or any other well-bred Hindoo think, when he peruses in our holy books the account of the immolating of creatures held most sacred by him? What will be his feelings, when he sees that the immolating of oxen and bulls constituted a leading feature in the religious ordinances of the Israelites, and that the blood of those most sacred animals was almost daily shed at the shrine of the god they adored? What will be his feelings when he sees, that after Solomon had at immense expense and labour built a magnificent temple in honour of the true God, he made the *pra-*

*tista* or consecration of it, by causing 22,000 oxen to be slaughtered, and overflowing his new temple with the blood of these sacred victims? He will certainly in perusing accounts, (in his opinion so horribly sacrilegious,) shudder, and be seized with the liveliest horror, look on the book containing such shocking details as an abominable work, (far be from me, once more, the blasphemy, I am expressing the feelings of a prejudiced Pagan,) throw it away with indignation, consider himself as polluted for having touched it, go immediately to the river for the purpose of purifying himself by ablutions from the defilement he thinks he has contracted, and before he again enters his house, he will send for a Poorohita Brahmin to perform the requisite ceremonies for purifying it from the defilement it has contracted, by ignorantly keeping within its walls so polluted a thing as the Bible.

In the mean while he will become more and more confirmed in the idea, that a religion which derives its tenets from so impure a source is altogether detestable, and that those who profess it, must be the basest and vilest of men.

Such are the effects which, in my humble opinion, the reading of the naked text of the

Bible cannot fail to produce on the unprepared minds of the prejudiced Hindoos.

I have only cited the above instances, being the first which occurred to my mind in writing this letter; but I could point out in almost every chapter of holy writ passages nearly as exceptionable, and which it would be equally dangerous to exhibit without a long previous explanation to the prejudiced Hindoo.

On the whole, it is my decided opinion, that to open all at once and without a long preparation, this precious treasure to the Hindoos, would be similar to attempting to cure a person labouring under severe sore eyes, by obliging him to stare at the rays of a shining sun, at the risk of rendering him altogether blind, or at least of being altogether dazzled and confounded by an excess of light. It would be the same as the administering of solid food to young babes, whilst their weak stomachs are hardly adequate to digest milk of the lightest kind; it is exactly (to use the language of the scriptures,) "to give that which is holy unto the dogs, and cast pearls before swine:" it is "to put wine into old bottles, which break, and the wine runneth out, and the bottles perish."

In order to give you an instance of the delicacy of the feelings of the natives, with respect to the accounts found in our holy books that are in opposition to their prejudices, I will relate the following occurrence:

Being at Carricaul, about twenty-eight years ago, I preached on a Sunday to the assembled congregation a sermon in the *Tamul* language, on the divine origin of the christian religion. Among other topics to prove my subject, I insisted on the intrinsic weakness and inadequacy of the means employed in the establishment of this religion, generally hated and persecuted everywhere, quite destitute of all human support, and left to its own resources amidst every kind of contradictions. I several times repeated, in treating this topic, that the christian religion had for its founder a *peasant of Galilee, the son of a humble carpenter*, who took for his assistants twelve low-born men, twelve ignorant and illiterate *fishermen*. These words *the son of a carpenter! twelve fishermen!* many times repeated, gave offence to my audience, which was entirely composed of native christians; and the sermon was no sooner finished than three or four of the principal among them came and informed me, that the whole congregation had been highly scandalized by hearing me apply to Christ the appellation of *the son of a car-*

*penter*, and to his apostles that of *fishermen*; that I could not be ignorant that the casts both of carpenters and fishermen were two of the lowest and vilest in the country; that it was highly improper to attribute to Christ and his disciples so low and abject an origin; that if pagans, who sometimes come through motives of curiosity to their religious assemblies, heard such objectionable accounts of our religion, their contempt and hatred of it would be considerably increased, &c. &c. Finally, they advised me, if in future I had occasion to mention in my sermons the origin of Christ or his apostles, not to fail to say that both were born in the noble tribe of *kshatrys* or rajahs, and never to mention their low profession.

Another instance of the kind happened to me a few years ago in this part of the country, when, in explaining to the congregation the parable of the Prodigal Son in the Gospel, I mentioned the circumstance of the prodigal's father having, through joy, killed the *fatted calf* to regale his friends, on account of the return of his reformed son. After the lecture some Christians told me, in rather bad humour, that my mentioning the *fatted calf* was very improper, and that if, as sometimes happened, pagans had been present at the lecture, they would have been confirmed, on hearing of the fattened calf, in the opinion they all entertained of the Christian religion being a low or pariah religion. They advised me, in the mean time, if in future I gave an explanation of the same parable, to substitute a lamb instead of the *fatted calf*.

In fact, even with our native Christians, we are careful to avoid all that might wound their feelings to no purpose, and increase in the public mind the jealousy and contempt entertained against them, and their religion. For example, as the use of intoxicating liquors is extremely odious to all well-bred Hindoos, and considered by them as a capital sin, when we explain verbally or in writing the sacrament of the eucharist, we are cautious not to say openly that the materials of this sacrament are bread and *wine*, or *charayam*, (literally, wine), which would prove too revolting to their feelings; we have therefore the precaution to soften this coarse term by a periphrasis, saying that the materials of the eucharist are wheaten bread, and *the juice of the fine fruit called grape*; which expressions become more palatable to their taste.

But should the translation of the Bible into the various languages of the country, and circulated among the Hindoos, be able, through their intrinsic worth, to overcome, by little and little, all their prejudices, and fix their attention to this divine book (which supposition I am far from admitting), a great difficulty would yet remain; that is, a close and accurate version of the work. All persons the least familiar with the dialects of the country and their style, will agree with me, I think, that they are so different from those of Europe, that a literal translation of the Holy Scriptures into any of them is impracticable.

I was not a little surprised when I saw, a few years ago, announced with much emphasis in all the newspapers by the missionaries at Serampore, the design of undertaking the translation of the whole into eighteen or twenty Asiatic languages, the Chinese not excepted. To persons unacquainted with the difficulty, not to say impossibility of such a task being faithfully and accurately performed, the project must have appeared dazzling and worthy to be encouraged: for my part, I could not conceive how a small society of five or six individuals (every allowance for their talents and learning being made,) should seriously think of compromising themselves with the public by so herculean a labour; which, to be fairly and properly executed, would occupy for half a century, all the learned to be found in India.

It is a well known fact, that when England separated herself from the church of Rome, not finding the version of the *Vulgate*, till then used, sufficiently exact, the first care of her reformers was to procure a translation of the whole Bible, from the original Hebrew into English. In consequence, one was produced with great trouble, in the reign of the young king Edward the Sixth; but this version, on a close investigation, proving abundant in errors, was finally laid aside, and a second undertaken in the reign of queen Elizabeth. This also could not withstand criticism, and was found, on the whole, very incorrect and defective; a third version was therefore begun in the reign of James the First, which (if I am not mistaken) is that now used and approved by the established church. In order to render this as exact and correct as it was possible, the best scholars to be found in the kingdom were employed in the execution of it, and it is well known that this version, carried on by the joint labours of so many learned persons, took up a period of about sixteen years, for its completion; and yet modern criticism has found many errors and mistakes in it, although obtained by so much trouble and care.

Now, if even in Europe, with all the assistance that learned translators were enabled to obtain, from enlightened criticism, &c. it proved so difficult, and required such great labours to obtain a genuine version of this work, what are we to think of the project of five or six individuals, who, without the assistance of any criticism whatever, suppose themselves able to execute genuine translations into intricate languages, with which they, after all, can possess only an imperfect acquaintance? *

* Since writing these pages, I have learned, with some surprise, that the missionaries at Serampore have surpassed the most sanguine expectations of the public, by translating the Scriptures, within the short period of nine or ten years, into no less than twenty-four Asiatic languages. This brilliant success has not in the least dazzled me, nor altered my opinion, or diminished my scepticism on the entire inadequacy of such means to enlighten the pagans, and gain them over to Christianity, and I would not certainly dare to warrant, that these twenty spurious versions, with some of which I am acquainted, will, after the lapse of the same number of years, have operated the conversion of twenty-four pagans. I have, on the contrary, every reason for apprehending that these low translations, if the natives could be prevailed upon to peruse them, (which, in my opinion, will never be the case,) will, by exposing the Christian religion and its followers to the ridicule of the public, soon stagger the wavering faith of many hundreds of those now professing

It is on all hands admitted, that before a translation from one language into another be undertaken, it is absolutely necessary to possess an entire and thoroughly grammatical acquaintance with both. Now, where are the Europeans who possess so perfect a knowledge of the idioms of India? and again, where are the natives who possess the same advantage with respect to the European dialects? if persons of this description are to be found any where in this country, they are in very small numbers indeed.

Some partial translations of the Scriptures are, it is true, to be found in the country; but in my humble opinion they have entirely missed their object. I have by me a copy of the New Testament, translated into Tamul, executed by the Lutheran missionaries; but the translators, by endeavouring to make it literal, have generally used such low, trivial, and, in many instances, ludicrous expressions, and the style is, besides, so different from that of the Hindoos, that persons unaccustomed to it, cannot (as I have witnessed in repeated instances) read over four verses without laugh-

---

Christianity, hasten the epoch of their apostacy, and accelerate the downfall of the tottering edifice of Christianity in India.

ing at the manner in which the work is executed.

In my last journey to the coast, I saw a letter on the subject, from a missionary in Travancore, to a person of the same description at Pondicherry, in which were the following expressions:—

"Many hundred sets of the New Testament, translated into the *Malayan* dialect, have been sent to us (without our asking for them), to be circulated among our Christians. I have perused this performance: the translation is truly piteous, and only worthy of contempt: one cannot peruse four verses without shrugging up the shoulders. This large collection of New Testaments now in our hands places us in a very aukward situation: if we leave them to rot in our apartments, we fear to expose ourselves to the displeasure of those who supplied us with them, who appear anxious to have them circulated, and if we follow their instructions on the subject, we cover ourselves with ridicule."

I remember an instance of the kind, which will not appear foreign to my subject. About twenty-five years ago, the French missionaries, in the province of Sutchuen in China, were earnestly requested by the congregation *De Propaganda Fide* at Rome to translate the

Gospel into Chinese, and send a copy to them. The missionaries answered, that as the Chinese language did not admit of a literal translation, they had, a long time before, compiled a work in Chinese containing the history and moral of the Gospel, for the use of their congregations, and that nothing more could be satisfactorily executed on the subject; yet, as the request was urgent, they prepared, with the assistance of their best informed proselytes, a translation of the gospel of St. Matthew, a copy of which they sent to Rome, informing, at the same time, the congregation *De Propaganda*, that the translation of this gospel alone, obtained with the assistance of many well-educated natives, had cost them considerable labour and trouble; adding, that this literal translation differed so widely from the Chinese style, that even their converts would hardly refrain from laughing in perusing it.

Now, it is not a little curious to observe that what European missionaries, who had passed the greatest part of their lives in China, judged next to impossible to execute even with the assistance of many well-educated natives, an unassisted Armenian, of the name of *Lassar* at Serampore, should imagine himself able to perform; and it is not only the translation of a single gospel he has undertaken,— the whole Bible literally translated by this individual has been emphatically promised by the missionaries to the curiosity of the public.

Many unprejudiced and unbiassed Europeans, acquainted with the idioms of the country, with whom I have had opportunities of conversing on the subject, and who happened to have perused some parts of the translations of the Scriptures now extant, I am happy to say, perfectly coincided in opinion with me, that such low and vulgar versions of our holy books ought carefully to be concealed from the sight of the pagans, in order that their aversion to Christianity may not be increased, and the European character injured.

In fact, a translation of the Holy Scriptures, in order to awaken the curiosity, and fix the attention of the learned Hindoo, at least as a literary production, ought to be on a level with the Indian performances of the same kind among them, and be composed in fine poetry, a flowery style, and a high stream of eloquence, this being universally the mode in which all Indian performances of any worth are written. As long as the versions are executed in the low style in which we find these, you may rest assured that they will only excite contempt, and tend to increase the aversion already entertained by the natives against the Christian religion.

But, to conclude, let Bibles, as many as you please, in every shape and in every style, be translated and circulated among the Hindoos; let them, if you wish, be spread in every village, in every cottage, in every family; let the Christian religion be presented to these people under every possible light, I repeat it with deep sorrow, in my humble opinion, (an opinion grounded on twenty-five years of experience,) the time of conversion has passed away, and, under existing circumstances, there remains no human possibility to bring it back.

The Christian religion has been announced to the natives of India, without intermission during the last three or four centuries, at the beginning with some faint hopes of success, but at present with no effect. In the mean time, the oracle of the Gospel has been fulfilled with respect to the Hindoos. The Divine Founder of our religion has, it is true, announced that his gospel *should be preached all over the world*, but, to the best of my knowledge, he has never affirmed that it should be heard, believed, and embraced by all nations.

This is not the place to enter into a discussion of the awful and unfathomable mystery of *predestination*, to scrutinize the apparently obscure ways of the Supreme Wisdom on this subject, to ask the common Father of mankind why, in his all-ruling providence he has vouchsafed to impart the heavenly light of his divine word only to a part of his children, whilst he has withheld this, the greatest of all divine favours, from the other part, and left them immersed in the deepest darkness of the most extravagant idolatry. The thing is so, therefore there must be reasons for its being so. "Who hath known the mind of the Lord? or who hath been his counsellor?" Let every one among us, with becoming humility, acknowledge, in what concerns him, the greatness of the gift, and preserve in his heart a due sense of gratitude for it, without presuming to investigate the apparent partiality of the Giver.

Has not St. Paul forcibly and satisfactorily answered this question, by the masterly manner in which he treats the subject of the gratuitous election of God, when writing to the Romans he says, "What shall we say then? Is there unrighteousness with God? God forbid! For he saith to Moses, I will have mercy on whom I will have mercy, and I will have compassion on whom I will have compassion.—Therefore hath he mercy on whom he will have mercy, and whom he will he hardeneth.—O man, who art thou that repliest against God? Shall the thing formed say to him that formed it, Why hast thou made me thus? Hath not the potter power over the clay, of the same lump to make one vessel unto honour, and another unto dishonour?"

But to return to our subject, and in support of what I have above stated, that Christ had nowhere promised that his divine religion should be unexceptionably embraced by all nations; but, that rather opposition to the evangelical truths on the part of several nations was foreseen by him. This will appear from his own sacred words; for in the admirable and truly divine instructions he gave to his disciples (Matt. x. Luke, x.), when he invested them with full powers to preach his divine religion to all people, and when he sent them on the work of proselytism, he warned them that they must be prepared to meet hatred, and in many instances open resistance. It is true that he utters, at the same time, dreadful threats against the obdurate unbelievers, who shall shut their ears to the word of God; but he takes upon himself the punishment of their obduracy on the day of retribution: all that he recommends his disciples in such circumstances is, not to be stiff or too troublesome, not to insist and strive to enforce by all means the impugned truth on the minds of their hearers; but rather to yield, to submit by a patient resignation and forbearance; quietly to quit the places and countries so ill disposed to hear the truth, and to leave these people in their hardness of heart: "And (says he) into whatever city or town you shall enter, enquire who in it is worthy; and there abide till ye go thence: and when ye go into an house, salute it, and if the house be worthy, let your peace come upon it; but if it be not worthy, let your peace return to you. And whosoever shall not receive you, nor hear your words, when you depart out of that house or city, take off the dust of your feet." (Or as Mark and Luke relate,) "Go your way into the streets, and say, Even the dust of your city, which cleaveth on us, we do wipe off against you. Verily I say unto you, It shall be more tolerable for the land of Sodom and Gomorrah, in the day of judgment, than for that city." (Matt. x. Mark, vi. Luke, ix. and x.)

Happy would it be, indeed, had the divine instructions given by Christ to his immediate disciples, in these chapters of his divine work, been followed by a great many of those styling themselves their successors. We should not now have to deplore the dreadful calamities which have convulsed the world for so long a period, nor the violent struggles which have deluged Europe with blood, by sacrilegiously abusing the name of a religion, which in every page of his divine code holds out peace, charity, benevolence, and forbearance.

That the apostles faithfully conformed themselves to these divine instructions, appears clearly from several passages of our holy books. The most zealous among them, *Paul*, having many times, by his insinuating eloquence, convinced the Jews assembled in their synagogues at Jerusalem, Antioch, and other places, of the truth of the Christian religion, in so masterly a manner as to draw upon himself their reluctant applauses, without, however, being able to overcome entirely their prejudices; nay, ending by having to encounter the hatred and open resistance of the zealots of the opposite party, confounded as they were at the sight of his virtues, and at his unrivalled eloquence. On such occasions, what does the apostle? He yields, he submits, he resigns himself, he conducts himself according to the rules laid down by his divine employer. Behold his conduct under such trying circumstances as related in the following passage:—

"But when the Jews saw the multitudes, they were filled with envy against those things, which were spoken by Paul, contradicting and blaspheming. Then Paul and Barnabas waxed bold, and said, It was necessary that the word of God should first have been spoken to you; but seeing you put it from you, and judge yourselves unworthy of everlasting life, lo, we turn to the Gentiles.—But they shook off the dust of their feet against them, and came into Iconium." (Acts, xiii.)

As a most sincere, and most undisguised believer of the divine origin of the Christian religion, and firmly persuaded that this religion alone can render man happy in this life, and in that to come, my most earnest wishes have always been to see it believed and professed by all mankind, and extend its dominion, its mild and genial influence, all over the world, and among all nations.

Some persons seem to be of opinion, that should the civil government of the country give proper support and encouragement to the Christian religion, it might be rescued from the state of contempt and degradation into which it has fallen, and prosper. In my humble opinion, this might have been the case in former times; but under existing circumstances, when the prejudices of the Hindoos against it have reached so great a height, I question whether all practicable support on the part of government could materially advance its interests, and whether such an interference would not rather prove detrimental to it, by increasing the jealousy and distrust of the natives.

Some others think that the intercourse of Europeans with the natives ought sooner or later to bring about a revolution in the religion and manners of the latter. But in order to produce such an effect, this intercourse ought to be more close, more intimate, and confidential than it is now or has ever been. Has the intercourse of the Mahometans with the Hindoos, during a period of nearly a thousand years, although more familiar than that which prevails between the latter and their European rulers, been able to bring about such a revolution, and overcome the prejudices of these people against all foreign institutions? and have the Mahometan rulers during so long a period made converts to their religion and manners, otherwise than by coercive and violent measures?

It is a well known fact, that it is precisely those of the Hindoos who are most familiar, and most connected with the Europeans, who manifest the strongest disgust and aversion for the religion and manners of the latter. In proof of this assertion, I appeal to all the officers, both civil and military, serving under the three presidencies in India. Have the latter never discovered among their numerous army a single sepoy, with perhaps the exception of a few drunkard drummers and pariahs, who shewed the remotest inclination to turn a Christian? and has any collector or judge, or other civil officer of rank, to boast to have found out a single native under his control, who was not prejudiced in a particular manner against the Christian religion and the European customs and education?

As for me, whenever I have been exposed to any contradiction in the public exercise of my religious duties, I have found that they always originated with the natives serving in a public capacity, in any of the offices of government, and never with the peaceable inhabitants of the country, among whom I have everywhere met with the greatest tolerance.

In my opinion, the Hindoos will remain the same in this respect, after another thousand years, as they were a thousand years ago. Their reserved and distant intercourse with Europeans, will always continue the same, and their abhorrence of the religion, education, and manners of the latter, as well as their other leading prejudices, will continue undiminished.

At the same time, should the intercourse between the individuals of both nations, by becoming more intimate and more friendly, produce a revolution in the religion and usages of the country; it will not be to turn Christians that they will forsake their own religion; but rather, (what in my opinion is a thousand times worse than idolatry,) to become perfect atheists; and if they renounce their present manners, it will not be to embrace those of the Europeans, but rather to become what are now called pariahs.

Such would be, in my humble opinion, the sad results of this revolution, if it were ever to take place.

I remain, &c. &c.

*August 7th*, 1815.

# LETTER II.

To the Rev. G. B.—*Bombay.*

My dear Sir,

SINCE I had the pleasure of seeing you at ———, having constantly journeyed from one place to another, on my visits to the several congregations of the native Christians living in this part of the country, I had until now no leisure to give you the abridged sketch you are anxious to have of the state of Christianity in these provinces, in addition to what I wrote before on the subject. I now take the first moments of leisure I can spare, to gratify your curiosity, and give you as far as my information goes, the further details you wish to have on this interesting topic.

I have nothing, or very little to add to what I stated in my former letter, concerning the few congregations of native Christians of the Lutheran persuasion. The management of those congregations has to these times been intrusted to the care of Lutheran missionaries, sent from Denmark and Germany, whose principal establishment was till now at Trankbar, from whence missionaries were sent to attend the subordinate congregations settled at Madras, Tanjore, and Trichinopoly.

The management of by far the more numerous congregations of Christians of the Roman catholic persuasion dispersed over the country, from the banks of Krishna to Cape Comorin, is intrusted to the superintendance of two titular archbishops, two titular bishops, and three bishops *in partibus*, with the title of apostolic vicars.

The two archbishops are those of Goa, the metropolitan of India, who also takes the title of primate of the East and of Cranganore on the Malabar coast. The latter has been vacant during the last forty years, and the archbishopric has during that period been administered by a general vicar, appointed by the archbishop of Goa.

The two bishopricks are those of St. Thomas near Madras, and Cochin, both vacant also during the last fifteen or sixteen years; the distracted state of Europe, and other circumstances, not having yet allowed the court of Portugal to fill up these three vacant sees. In the interval, the two latter have been administered, as well as the former, by general vicars, appointed by the metropolitan archbishop of Goa, who is at present the only survivor among the four titular bishops in India.

These four bishops were at all times appointed by the court of Portugal, which always claimed the exclusive right of patronage over the religious affairs of India, and endeavoured to prevent the catholic missionaries of other countries from being sent to Asia on the work of proselytism, judging itself alone adequate to the undertaking, and using all the means in its power, after having lost its once formidable temporal influence in the country, to preserve in it a kind of spiritual authority, and an absolute and exclusive monopoly in the conversion of the heathens, the salvation of souls, and the opening of the gates of heaven.

However, these pretended rights were overlooked by the Holy See, which, from the beginning, used its paramount authority in spiritual matters, and in spite of the often-repeated protestations of the court of Portugal on the subject, appointed bishops *in partibus*, with the title of apostolic vicars, in several parts of Asia, under the immediate control of the congregation *de propaganda* at Rome, and quite independent of the titular bishops appointed by the court of Portugal.

These apostolic vicars, holding their religious authority from the congregation *De Propaganda*, are three in number in this peninsula. One is settled at Bombay, another at Verapoly near Cochin, and the third at Pondicherry; each of them has a small body of missionaries, both Europeans and natives, to visit and attend the congregations under their control. The European missionaries are at present few in number, and all old or infirm, as the distracted state of Europe, during these past twenty-five years, did not allow new supplies of persons of this description being sent to Asia. On this account the missions are threatened with a speedy extinction; the native clergy being altogether unqualified to preserve them, if left to their own resources, and deprived of the countenance of the European missionaries.

You therefore see that there are in all seven catholic bishops in India to manage the interests of the Roman catholic worship.

To commence with the archbishop of Goa, he has under his jurisdiction the largest number of Christians of all descriptions. I have been credibly informed, that the aggregate number amounted to 300,000 souls; and when it is considered that two-thirds at least of the population in the Portuguese establishments are Christians, and that out of 160,000 to be found in the Island of Ceylon, two-thirds are of the catholic persuasion*, under the jurisdiction of the archbishop of Goa, I am led to believe that this number is not exaggerated.

The archbishop has a native clergy, educated in the seminaries at Goa, and composed, I have been told, of about 1,500 priests, monks, and friars.

After the archbishop of Goa, comes next in rank the archbishop of Cranganore, a see still vacant. This mission was once flourishing, and seventy or eighty years back it reckoned under its jurisdiction, which extended to Madura and other countries, to the very shores of the Krishna, above 200,000 native Christians. At the present time, for the reasons stated in another letter, the number is reduced to about a third of this number.

The bishopric of Cochin contains a little more that 60,000 Christians.

The bishopric of St. Thomas near Madras, has under its jurisdiction about 50,000 Christians, natives, and half-castes.

Among the three apostolic vicars, who are

* The remainder are Calvinists, attended by the Dutch Calvinist missionaries.

independent of the titular bishops, the bishop of Bombay has the least numerous mission, all the Christians under his jurisdiction not exceeding 10 or 12,000, chiefly half-castes. This mission is attended by Italian Carmelite friars.

The apostolic vicar at Pondicherry exercises his spiritual jurisdiction over the Carnatic and Mysore, in which countries are to be found about 35,000 Christians.

The mission under the control of the apostolic vicar of Verapoly near Cochin, is also attended by Italian Carmelites, and is the most flourishing of the three. It chiefly extends in the Travancore country. This mission reckons 120,000 Christian natives, immediately attended by about a hundred native priests, educated by the Carmelites, now three or four in number, in their seminary at Verapoly. It has under its jurisdiction Syriac and Latin priests to officiate in the congregations of both rites, settled in the Travancore country. It is at present the only mission in which converts are still made amongst the heathen inhabitants. I have it from good authority, that between three and four hundred pagans are yearly christened in it, and that this number might be increased, were the missionaries to possess adequate means for the purpose. The principal cause of such extraordinary success, which is not to be met with elsewhere in India, is the following: —

The Travancore country is chiefly inhabited by the tribe of *Nairs*, who are of all Hindoos the most particular and severe in the observation of their usages and domestic regulations, and who, for the most trifling transgressions of these, expel the offenders from the caste. These outlawed persons being left without help in society after their expulsion, and shunned by all as degraded men, are under the necessity of forming new connexions, and have no other resource left for the purpose, than that of becoming converts to Christianity or Mahometanism. The greater part prefer the latter, the Mahometan religion holding out to them greater temporal advantages, and not imposing on them so many restraints as Christianity.

As I am speaking of the Christians living in Travancore, this will be the place to give you such information as I possess, upon the till now supposed *Nestorian congregations* settled in that country, who boast themselves to be the offspring of the converts made there by the Apostle St. Thomas.

Several, and in many respects contradictory accounts of this sect have of late been published, some writers supposing them *Nestorians*, and others asserting them to be *Eutychians*. But the fact is, that they do not know themselves to what sect they belong. The disturbances which have arisen among themselves during these last two centuries, have rendered them so unsettled in their religious tenets, that you will scarcely find the most intelligent among them agreeing in the exposition of their faith. It appears however, from the best information I have been able to obtain on the subject, that they are divided into two sects, a part being Nestorians, and another part Eutychians.

However, there is little room to doubt, that when they were first visited by the jesuit missionaries about two centuries ago, they all were found obstinately to adhere to the tenets professed by *Nestorius*, whose errors, condemned at first in the general council of Ephesus, and afterwards in that of Chalcedon, when renewed by *Dioscorus*, were the subject of so many controversies in the church, from the sixth to the end of the eighth centuries.

Their chief error relates to the mystery of incarnation. They reject the authority of the first four general councils, which are the first council of Nice, the first of Constantinople, that of Ephesus, and that of Chalcedon, in which councils, the Christian faith about the incarnation was clearly defined and vindicated against the new-fangled doctrines of Arius, Nestorius, Eutychus and other sectaries; and their leading error was, to admit with Nestorius, a single nature and two distinct persons in Christ; while the Eutychians acknowledge two natures and two persons.

They above all deny the Blessed Virgin the title of *Theo-tocus*, or *Mother of God*, asserting that the Son of God did not assume a soul and a body in her womb.

This sect has preserved the ecclesiastical hierarchy, consisting among them of a patriarch, bishops, and an inferior clergy. The Nestorians own obedience in religious matters to the patriarch of Babylon, and the Eutychians are said to acknowledge the authority of the patriarch of Antioch. Their bishops derive their authority from either, and they ordain the inferior clergy by the imposition of hands.

They admit seven sacraments, in common with the catholic church. They have the mass, and admit the real presence of Christ in the eucharist. They have not the auricular confession, but they admit purgatory, prayers for the dead, and invocation of saints.

They have numberless fasts during the

course of the year; they use candles, tapers, incense, and have many more external ceremonies than the catholics in the exercise of their religious functions; but they altogether reject the worship of images, except the bare cross, which is set up in all their churches, and to which they pay worship. Their waste of frankincense is very considerable, as they perform no religious ceremonies in their churches and at home, without being surrounded by clouds of smoke of incense.

Their clergy lived till lately in celibacy; but I have heard that some protestant missionaries had recently prevailed upon many of them to marry, and that it was the only success they had to boast of.

The Catholic, Nestorian, and Eutychian clergy among them use the Syriac in their liturgy and religious ceremonies; but as all their learning on the subject consists in the ability to spell it, without understanding it, I cannot see of what utility your project of supplying them with Syriac Bibles could be. No one among them is capable of understanding that ancient language.

Besides the above mentioned missions, there is another at Madras, under the direction of Italian capuchins, having for their superior an apostolic prefect, and holding their spiritual powers from the congregation *De Propaganda.* This mission contains ten or twelve thousand Christians of several descriptions, natives, half-castes, &c. living at Madras and its vicinity.

The same Italian capuchins endeavoured also to form religious establishments in the provinces of Bengal, Oude, Bahar, &c. They penetrated as far as Nepal and Thibet; but they met with only trifling success in those several countries. They had formerly a small congregation in Nepal, and they have still chapels at Agra, Lucknow, Patna, and three or four other places in the province of Bahar; but their places of worship in these several countries are very thinly attended, and the few people who frequent them are chiefly half-castes.

In fact, it has been remarked that the prejudices to be met with every where among the Hindoos, and which at every period proved an insurmountable obstacle to the introduction of the Christian religion in India, were still more deeply rooted in the provinces bordering upon the Ganges than elsewhere. In more favourable times the congregation *De Propaganda* sent successively several bodies of missionaries to that country, in order to diffuse over it at least some gleams of the evangelical light. The French jesuits, the Portuguese Augustinians, the Italian capuchins, were sent in succession for that purpose; but they could make no impression; at last all their endeavours proving abortive, and being baffled in all their attempts, the undertaking was laid aside.

I have made no mention in this sketch of the Armenian clergy settled at Madras, because they at no time attempted to make proselytes among the Hindoos, and their only business has always been to attend the Armenian congregation settled at that place. This sect of Christians does not disagree very much in its religious tenets with the catholic church. Indeed the only substantial difference I was able to remark, is, that their clergy are allowed the state of marriage, and that they reject the supremacy of the pope, acknowledging allegiance only to a patriarch of their own, in spiritual matters; for the rest, they profess nearly the same faith as the catholics, admitting in common with them, the seven sacraments, the mass, transubstantiation, the worship of images, invocation of saints, &c. &c. Their liturgy is in the Armenian language.

From this short general sketch of the several missions in the peninsula, you will perceive that the number of Neophites, although reduced to no more than a third of what it was about seventy years ago, is yet considerable; and it would afford some consolation, if at least a due proportion amongst them were real and unfeigned Christians. But, alas! this is far from being the case. The greater, the by far greater number, exhibit nothing but a vain phantom, an empty shade of Christianity. In fact, during a period of twenty five years that I have familiarly conversed with them, lived among them as their religious teacher and spiritual guide, I would hardly dare to affirm that I have any where met a sincere and undisguised Christian.

In embracing the Christian religion, they very seldom heartily renounce their leading superstitions, towards which they always entertain a secret bent, which does not fail to manifest itself in the several occurrences of life; and in many circumstances where the precepts of their religion are found to be in opposition to their leading usages, they rarely scruple to overlook the former, and conform themselves to the latter.

Besides, in order to make true Christians among the natives, it would be necessary before all things, to erase from the code of the Christian religion, the great leading precept of *charity*; for try to persuade a Hindoo that this religion places all men on equal footing in the sight of God, our common Maker and Father; —that the being born in a high caste, authorizes nobody to look with indifference or contempt on the persons born in a lower tribe;—that even the exalted Brahmin, after embracing Christianity, ought to look upon the humble pariah as his brother, and be ready to bestow upon him all marks of kindness and love in his power;—try to prevail upon the christian Hindoo to forgive an often imaginary injury, such as would be that of being publicly upbraided with having violated any one of their vain usages;—try to persuade even the low-born pariah, that after turning a Christian, he ought for ever to renounce the childish distinction of *Right and Left Hand*, upon which he lays so much stress, and which he considers as the most honourable characteristic of his tribe;—tell him that as that distinction of *Right and Left Hand* proves a source of continual quarrel, fighting, and animosity, it becomes wholly incompatible with the first duties imposed upon him by the Christian religion, and must altogether be laid aside;—try to prevail upon parents, in opposition to the established customs, to permit a young widow, their daughter, who, on account of her youth, is exposed to dishonor, both herself and family, to marry again; so to act in opposition to any of their leading usages and practices; your lectures, your instructions, your expostulations on such subjects, will be of no avail; and your Christians will continue to live the slaves of their Antichristian prejudices and customs.

When their religious instructors become too troublesome to them, by their importunate admonitions on such subjects, they often put themselves in a state of insurrection, revolt against them, and bid them defiance, by threats of apostacy.

On the other hand, the practical virtues of Christianity are almost unknown to them. Many among them are tolerably well acquainted with the doctrine and morality of their religion; but by far the greater number live in the grossest ignorance on these points, and the religion of all consists in little more than a few outward practices, and the occasional recital of some forms of prayer, accompanied, it is true, with many external grimaces, but without any inward or practical spirit of religion. Indeed, all their exercises are either a mere routine, or practised from a respect to appearances, so as not to be exposed by too marked a negligence to the animadversions of their religious guides, rather than from a consciousness of duty towards God.

The Hindoos are a people so peculiarly circumstanced, that I consider it next to impossibility to make among them real and sincere Christians. The force of prejudice is known to all; and every one knows, also, that no people in the earth were ever such slaves to education and customs as they are. It is well known, also, that the introduction of any new usages and regulations, either religious or civil, among them, has at all times baffled the utmost endeavours of all their fierce conquerors, their attachment to their own institutions has always been invincible, and their horror of every novelty insurmountable.

The Hindoos are a people entirely different from all others. You may, if you choose, exercise over them the most despotic sway; you may oppress them by every kind of tyranny; you may overload them with taxes, and rob them of their property; you may carry away their wives and children, load them with chains and send them into exile:—to all such excesses they will perhaps submit; but if you speak of changing any of their principal institutions, either religious or civil, you will find a quite ungovernable people, never to be overcome on this point; and it is my decided opinion, that the day when government shall presume to interfere in such matters, will be the last of its political existence.

This force of custom is remarked among the native Christians, as well as among the pagans. The former shew in all their religious concerns an apathy or insensibility, a dullness bordering in most instances on stupidity. Indeed, the education of all Hindoos renders them incapable of acquiring new ideas, and every thing which varies from the established customs is rather odious, or at least indifferent to them. It is not that they want wit, penetration, and aptness in the matters in which they were brought up, or those in which their temporal interests are compromised; but it is impossible to instil new principles, or infuse new ideas into their minds.

Besides that, surrounded on all sides by a religion which speaks to the senses, allures and bewilders its votaries by all kinds of sensual gratifications in this life, and in that which is to come, their minds are too gross to understand a religion which speaks only to the spirit, exhibits to them only inscrutable mysteries, and promises them chiefly spiritual enjoyments.

The Hindoos are constituted in such a manner by their education and customs, that they are quite insensible to all that does not make a strong impression on the senses. Fully aware of their dispositions, the impostors who contrived their monstrous form of worship, consulted in doing so the peculiar temper and character of these nations, and as they had to deal with a people who, they perceived, were only to be stirred up and roused by monstrosities, they in consequence gave to them a monstrous religion.

In fact, in discoursing upon the Christian religion with the Hindoos, your hearers will readily agree with you upon all that you say; but they will feel nothing. When you discourse upon such topics, either among the Christians or pagans, your hearers sitting down on their heels, or cross-legged, will patiently, and with frequent assenting nods listen to you. But after preaching to them in this manner for several days, ask them for an account of your sermons, or moral instructions, and you will find that they have comprehended nothing, and that you have laboured in vain, because instead of speaking to their senses, you endeavoured to speak to their minds.

Seeing the empire of the senses over these

people, and that their imagination was only to be roused by strongly moving objects, the first missionaries among them judged that some advantage might result to the cause of religion by accommodating themselves, as far as possible, to their dispositions. Agreeably to this idea, the ordinary pomp and pageantry which attend the catholic worship, so objectionable to the protestant communions in general, were not judged by them striking enough to make a sufficient impression on the gross minds of the Hindoos. They in consequence incumbered the catholic worship with an additional superstructure of outward shew, unknown in Europe, which in many instances does not differ much from that prevailing among the gentiles, and which is far from proving a subject of edification to many a good and sincere Roman catholic.

This Hindoo pageantry is chiefly seen in the festivals celebrated by the native Christians. Their processions in the streets, always performed in the night time, have indeed been to me at all times a subject of shame. Accompanied with hundreds of *tom-toms*, (small drums,) trumpets, and all the discordant noisy music of the country; with numberless torches, and fire-works: the statue of the saint placed on a car which is charged with garlands of flowers, and other gaudy ornaments, according to the taste of the country, —the car slowly dragged by a multitude shouting all along the march—the congregation surrounding the car all in confusion, several among them dancing, or playing with small sticks, or with naked swords: some wrestling, some playing the fool; all shouting, or conversing with each other, without any one exhibiting the least sign of respect or devotion. Such is the mode in which the Hindoo Christians in the inland country celebrate their festivals. They are celebrated, however, with a little more decency on the coast. They are all exceedingly pleased with such a mode of worship, and any thing short of such pageantry, such confusion and disorder, would not be liked by them.

I at several times strove to make those within my range sensible of the unreasonableness of so extravagant a worship, and how opposite it was to true piety; but my admonitions proving every where a subject of scandal rather than of edification to my hearers, who in several instances went so far as to suspect the sincerity of my faith, and to look upon me as a kind of free-thinker, and a dangerous innovator, merely on account of my free remarks on the subject, I judged it more prudent to drop the matter, and overlook abuses it was out of my power to suppress. I cannot but declare that the necessity under which I stood to wink at such, and (in my opinion) many other no less reprehensible abuses, proved to me at all times a subject of great vexation and disgust.

I may perhaps appear to many, too severe in my criticism of the processions, and other outward ceremonies performed by the Hindoo Christians. Some persons of my profession, for whose talents and virtues I entertain the utmost regard, with whom I discussed *the subject*, and to whom I frankly expressed my undisguised dislike of such pageantry, differed entirely from me in their view of the *case*, and asserted that in this circumstance, as in every other, a due allowance ought to be made for the education, the character, and the genius of the Hindoos; of a carnal people who were entirely enslaved to the empire of the senses, and whose imagination was only to be roused by strongly moving objects, &c. Their opinion may be right, and mine wrong. In support of their opinion, it might be said that our holy books afford us instances of solemn processions performed in the streets among *the chosen people*, which on the whole, according to our modern ideas of decorum, would appear to us no less objectionable than those of the Hindoo Christians. We have a full account of one of those processions, on the occasion of the transferring of the ark from the house of Abinadab, to that of Obe-dedom, and from thence to the city of David. (2 *Sam.* c. 6.—1 *Chron.* c. 15.) David and all the people were assembled for the occasion. The ark placed on a new car made for the purpose; "and David, and all the house of Israel, played before the Lord on all manner of instruments made of fir-wood, even on harps and psalteries, and on timbrels, and on cornets, and on cymbals," &c. &c. The holy king himself, over-powered with joy, and forgetting the gravity and decorum due to his exalted rank, "danced with all his might before the Lord," &c. "So David, and all the house of Israel, brought up the ark of the Lord *with shouting*, and with the sound of the trumpet," &c. &c.

In the mean time, the tolerating of such abuses, partly contrived, it appears, to allure the gentiles, by making an adequate impression on their senses, has missed its object; all this pageantry is at present beheld with indifference by the Hindoos, and the interests of the Christian religion have not been improved by what some may be disposed to term mere priest-craft.

If any one among the pagans still shews a desire to turn Christian, it is ordinarily among out-casts, or quite helpless persons, left without resources or connections in society, that they are to be found. They, generally speaking, ask for baptism from interested motives. Few, if any of these new converts, would be found, who might be said to have embraced Christianity from conviction; and I have every reason to apprehend, that as long as the usages and customs of the Hindoos continue unimpaired, it is perfect nonsense to think of making among them true and sincere proselytes.

In order to give you a striking idea of the religious dispositions of the Hindoo, and as a strong instance of what I asserted above, that there was to be found among them, nothing else but a vain phantom of Christianity, without any real or practical faith, I will with shame and confusion quote the following scandalous instance.

When the late Tippoo Sultan sought to extend his own religious creed all over his dominions, and make by little and little all the inhabitants in Mysore converts to Islamism, he wished to begin this fanatical undertaking with the native Christians living in his country, as the most odious to him, on the score of their religion. In consequence, in the year 1784, he gave secret orders to his officers in the different districts, to make the most diligent inquiries after the places where Christians were to be found, and to cause the whole of them to be seized on the same day, and conducted under strong escorts to Seringapatam. This order was punctually carried into execution; very few of them escaped, and I have it from good authority, that the aggregated number of the persons seized in this manner, amounted to more than 60,000.

Some time after their arrival at Seringapatam, Tippoo ordered the whole to undergo the rites of circumcision, and be made converts to Mahometanism. The Christians were put together during the several days that the ceremony lasted: and, oh shame!—oh scandal!—will it be believed in the Christian world?—no one, not a single individual among so many thousands, had courage enough to confess his faith under this trying circumstance, and become a martyr to his religion. The whole apostatized *en masse*, and without resistance, or protestations, tamely underwent the operation of circumcision; no one among them possessing resolution enough to say, "I am a Christian, and I will die rather than renounce my religion!"

So general a defection, so dastardly an apostacy, is, I believe, unexampled in the annals of Christianity.

After the fall of the late Tippoo Sultan, most of those apostates came back to be reconciled to their former religion, saying that, their apostacy had been only external, and they always kept in their hearts the true faith in Christ. About 2,000 of them fell in my way, and nearly 20,000 returned to the Mangalore district, from whence they had been carried away, and rebuilt there their former places of worship. God preserve them all from being exposed in future to the same trials; for should this happen, I have every reason (notwithstanding their solemn protestations when again reconciled to Christianity) to apprehend the same sad results, that is to say, a tame submission, and a general apostacy.

I have yet said nothing of that class of Christians in India commonly designated Portuguese, although most of them have no more relation by birth, or otherwise, to that people, or to any other European nation, than to the Tartar Calmucks. They are partly composed of half castes, the illegitimate offspring of Europeans, and a few descendants of the Portuguese; whilst the majority of them are the offspring of Hindoos of the lowest rank, who, after learning some one of the European dialects, put on a hat, boots, and the European dress, and endeavour to copy European manners. In my humble opinion, and as far as I can judge from my personal observations, this class of Indians, composed of catholics and protestants, is in many respects inferior to the other classes of society. It has been remarked, (I apprehend with truth,) by many observers of the character of these people, that most of them possessed the vices and bad qualities, both of Europeans and Hindoos, with but very few of the virtues and good qualities of either; and that amply stored with the laziness, apathy, and indolence of the natives, they, on the other hand, were destitute of the spirit of temperance and sobriety, self-command, patience and forbearance of the Hindoos, and also of that dignity and independence of mind which characterizes Europeans in the several circumstances of life.

The causes of such an inferiority are above all a neglected education, bad examples, and bad company. Most of them are born of a pagan, a Moorish, or a Pariah woman, or of a common prostitute, under whose tuition they remain to the age of 12 or 15 years. If a small proportion of them be sent to the public schools under the protection of government, where care is taken to give them a Christian education, many go to them after their morals have been already corrupted, and their manners thoroughly vitiated by the early bad education, and still worse examples of their parents, and heathen servants; and yet, the greater number cannot have the advantage of those public schools, and are in consequence fostered at home under the tuition of a Pariah concubine, and attendants of the lowest description, who instil into the minds of those youths all the vices peculiar to themselves, and leave their rising passions without control. We must, therefore, cease to be surprised at the looseness of manners, and other irregularities exhibited by this class of Indians. They generally live in distressed circumstances, and most of them are considerably in debt. The causes of their poverty are the vices peculiar to themselves; above all, a want of foresight, a love of show, and a spirit profusion, is common to all.

Some well wishers to this class of Indians have thought that the circulation of bibles among them was alone sufficient to produce the wished-for improvement in their condition, and I have many times been requested to lend my assistance for the purpose. I beg leave to observe, that among the native Christians,

Portuguese, or others, most of whom are immersed in the grossest ignorance on the subject of religion, it is not bibles which are wanted, but rather elementary works, such as catechisms, short and familiar instructions, plain explanations of the creed, of the ten commandments, simple lectures upon Christian duties, upon the principal virtues, upon charity, temperance, self-command, the forgiveness of injuries, &c. &c.

After having prepared their mind by such elementary works, the reading of the Holy Scriptures, chiefly the New Testament, would become more intelligible and useful. But if you begin to exhibit all at once, without previous preparation, the naked text of the Bible to their uncouth and ignorant mind, you will, in my humble opinion, derive very little advantage; no more indeed than from shewing light to a dim-sighted person before removing the opacity which prevents his organs from seeing clearly.

In fact, from what I have already stated, you will easily perceive, that all classes of Indians must be treated as mere children in matters of religion. They must, therefore, be fed with milk of the lighest kind. If you hazard to give them all at once solid food, their weak stomach will reject the whole, and their constitution, instead of being improved, will on the contrary be deteriorated, and entirely ruined by the frequently repeated experiment.

When I said that the class of Hindoos known under the appellation of Portuguese was inferior to the rest, I wished it to be understood that I only meant the majority of them; and this censure admits of very numerous exceptions. A great many, indeed, are to be found among them, whose minds have been cultivated by an early good education, and who conspicuously distinguish themselves from the others in society by their morals, the purity of their manners, their industry, their general deportment, and some by their gentleman-like conduct. But even in these you will always discover something Indian. They can never divest themselves entirely of that apathy, indolence, and dullness which seem to be the unavoidable lot of all people born under a vertical sun; and in spite of all their endeavours to imitate the Europeans, something is always remarked in them which discovers their origin, and seems to justify the old saying of Horace —

"Naturam expellas furcâ, tamen usque recurret.!"

The surest mode of improving the condition of this too much neglected class of Indians, which is daily increasing, would be in my humble opinion to give them more encouragement to excite their emulation by promoting the most worthy and best disposed among them to places and situations which many of them could occupy with ability, and which could render them respectable in society. At the present time, to add to the other sources of discouragement, they live despised by all, and almost forgotten. Spurned by the Europeans, spurned by the natives, who decline every familiar and confidential intercourse with them, they are necessarily thrown into a state of despair, which cannot fail to deaden in them all noble sentiments, and all kind of emulation.

From this picture of the state of Christianity in India, you will perceive how very trying must be the profession of a missionary in that country, and to how many dangers he is exposed in the arduous discharge of his professional duties, among a people so circumstanced, lying often, as he does, under the sad necessity of winking at their reprehensible practices, and overlooking usages which his conscience reprobates. You will also, I believe, agree with me, that of all professions this is the most distressing, and that much more than an ordinary share of resolution and courage is required to persevere in it.

What I have stated, will, I think, be sufficient to enable you not only to judge of the state of Christianity in India, but also of its very inadequate influence on the minds of those who have embraced it. I am, however, far from adopting the opinion of those who think that in such circumstances, and with a people of such dispositions, Christianity is of no avail at all; for, should it produce no other effect than that of altogether detaching so many thousand natives from the worship of idols, and the monstrous kind of idolatry prevailing all over India, to inculcate into their minds even nothing else but the merely barren and speculative knowledge of only one true God, and that of his only son our Lord and common Redeemer Jesus Christ; this alone, ought, in my humble opinion, to be sufficient to wish for, and encourage its diffusion by all practicable means. Such means, however, will, I fear, never be found, while the Hindoos are fettered by their prevailing institutions, and above all, by that relating to the distinction of castes; this alone will always prove an insurmountable bar to the conversion of the gentiles, and baffle the utmost efforts of the most zealous well-wishers to the cause of Christianity; and the very same causes which prevent us from improving the religious condition of the unfortunate Hindoos, will also, I apprehend, baffle all the efforts of a humane and benevolent government to improve, (at least in any material degree) their temporal interests.

I am still farther from admitting the bold opinion of many prejudiced or misinformed Europeans, who contend that the native Christians are the worst of all Hindoos. There is something savouring of blasphemy in this assertion; for, should that be the case, it would tend to nothing less than to prove that the Christian religion, so far from improving the condition of man, renders him on the contrary worse than pagans.

That on account of the peculiar prejudices under which all natives in India stand, it has but a very inadequate influence on their morals, manners, and general behaviour, will appear from what I have already stated. That most of them have nothing more of a Christian than the name, and, if not worse, are not yet much better than pagans, I am very reluctantly forced to admit; but that the Christian religion renders those who have embraced it worse than the worshippers of idols, is an untenable paradox, contradicted by experience; and will, I trust, be disavowed by every candid and impartial observer: and I must add, in justice to truth, that I am acquainted with many among them who are in their morals, probity, and general behaviour, irreproachable men, enjoying the confidence even of the pagans; and into whose hands I should not hesitate to intrust my own interests.

This statement will, I think, be sufficient to make it appear that my profession has not biassed my judgment on the subject, or rendered me over-partial to the Hindoo Christians; but notwithstanding all this, it is my opinion that if a parallel for honesty and probity were drawn between them and pagans, the former would have the advantage.

I will refrain from entering into details on the low state of Christianity among the Europeans living in this country, as this part of the subject is your province rather than mine. I will content myself with saying, that if their public and national virtues are a subject of praise and admiration to all the castes of Hindoos, the bare-faced immorality, the bad examples, and disregard of every sense of religion exhibited by a great many amongst them, are not the least among the many obstacles which oppose the progress of their religion in this country, by increasing the prejudices of the natives against it, and rendering it particularly odious to them, when they see it so ill observed by those who were educated in her bosom, and who come from countries where this religion alone is publicly professed. They think that there can be no advantage in embracing a religion which seems to have so little influence on the conduct of those who profess it: nay, a great many among them, judging from outward appearances, question whether the Europeans living among them have any religion whatever. I have been many times challenged to bear testimony on this fact, and very seriously asked by them whether the Frangy (Europeans) acknowledged and worshipped a God.

The causes just mentioned unfortunately operate very powerfully on the minds of the native Christians themselves, and by confounding and staggering their wavering faith, occasion the apostacy of many.

This, dear Sir, is an abridged sketch of the low and abject state of the Christian religion in India. In such discouraging circumstances, without any apparent human means to improve the cause of Christianity in this country, there only remains to the persons of our profession to look up with calmness and resignation to Him who holds in his hands the hearts of men, changes them when he pleases, and *is able, even of stones, to raise up children to Abraham,* when the time appointed by him for the purpose arrives.

In these deplorable times, in which scepticism and immorality threaten to overwhelm every nation, and every condition, it only remains to us *to weep, between the porch and the altar,* over the iniquities of the people; to water the sanctuary with our tears; to bewail, like Jeremiah, the general corruption; to edify the people by our lessons and examples; to look to the Father of mercies; to pray to him to bring about better times; *to spare his people, and not to give his heritage to reproach:* and if our interposition cannot stem the torrent, and our altars are finally to be overthrown by the sacrilegious hands of modern philosophy, let us have, as our last resource, resolution and fortitude enough to stand by them to the last, and allow ourselves to be crushed down, and buried under their ruins.

I have the honour to be, &c. &c. &c.

*December,* 1815.

# LETTER III.

To the Rev. G. B.—*Bombay.*

My dear Sir,

As in our last interview you were so kind as to say that you would, at all times, be glad to receive any farther communication I might wish to make on the state of Christianity in India, and the means, (if any existed,) of improving Christian knowledge in this country, in addition to what I formerly wrote on the subject, I indulge the hope that the new elucidations I am about to give will meet with your favourable reception.

I will chiefly insist on the two leading topics already treated in my former letters, and which have attracted the attention of well-wishers to the cause of Christianity; viz. Are there any human means of improving christian religion among the Hindoos?—Will the Holy Scriptures translated and circulated among them, by fixing their attention to this sacred book, awaken their curiosity, and excite in them a spirit of enquiry, or a desire to know the truth?

I must confess that, whenever I reflect upon this subject, I cannot help experiencing feelings of regret and despondency. The experience I have gained through a familiar intercourse with the natives of all castes, for a period of twenty-five years entirely passed in their society, during which I lived like themselves, conforming to their customs and prejudices, in order to gain their confidence, and endeavouring by these means to insinuate myself among them as a religious teacher, has made me thoroughly acquainted with the insuperable obstacles that Christianity will ever have to encounter in the deep-rooted and quite invincible prejudices, and in the invariable usages, customs, and education of the Hindoos of all castes; and it is my decided opinion, that not only the interests of the Christian religion will never be improved among them, but also that it will by little and little lose the small ground it had gained in better times; and, in a short period, dwindle away to nothing.

The Hindoos may be divided into two classes—the impostors, and the dupes. The latter include the bulk of the population of India; and the former is composed of the whole tribe of Brahmins. Now, in a society composed of such materials, we can entertain but very faint hopes of improving the interests, or extending the benefits of the Christian religion.

The Brahmins, in framing their system of imposture, and in devising the monstrous worship prevailing all over India, not only used every artifice in their power to adapt it to the dispositions of a simple and credulous people, but, above all, they employed all possible means to establish in this way, in a permanent and indisputable manner, the high power and uncontroverted control they have always exercised over the other tribes. In order that their artifice in establishing throughout the body of society the most downright imposture which ever prevailed among any nation on the earth, might not be questioned, they had the precaution to incumber the people with those numberless institutions, which, at the same time that they secure the permanent superiority of the Brahmins, render the other tribes incapable of reasoning, or of any mental exertion which might enable them to emerge from that state of intellectual degradation in which they are held by their unchangeable usages and customs.

It is indeed, it may be remarked, true that all impostors who introduced or propagated false religions contrived to answer only human and temporal purposes in the world, and when the leaders of the popular faith had recourse to the same artifices with the Hindoo Brahmins, and used, in common with them, every kind of cunning and craft to prevent the people from discovering their imposture, their end was the same; and that it is peculiar to the Christian religion to lay open to all, both friend and foe, its documents, its records and principles; because, this alone being founded on truth, this alone can boldly challenge the enquiries and attacks of the severest criticism, both ancient and modern.

To this I will answer, that no one among the contrivers and leaders of false religions was ever able to devise so well-framed a system of imposture as the Brahmins have done, in order to preserve unimpaired their religious control over the other castes, and to keep the latter in that state of stupidity and ignorance in which they are immersed. It is a sin, it is a crime, a sacrilege in every Hindoo who is not born a Brahmin to endeavour to emerge from that state of ignorance, and to aspire to the lowest degree of knowledge. It is a sin for him even to presume to calculate on what days fall the new and full moon. He is obliged to learn this and similar matters, and to be guided in the most common occurrences of life by his religious teachers. He is forbidden by his institutions to lay any claim whatever to either sacred or profane science, or to intermeddle in any way with the one or the other. His religious leaders have engrossed, as their absolute and exclusive inheritance, all that is included within the term *science*, fearing lest if an access, even to profane science, were given to the other tribes, this, by causing them to exert their own reason and judgment, should lead them to discover the heap of religious absurdities and extravagancies imposed upon their credulity by an interested priesthood.

Among the arts, the Brahmins have left to the other castes only those whose exercise depends more upon bodily than on mental exertion; such as, music on windy instruments, painting, sculpture, and mechanics; and even these they have beset with so many sources of discouragement, that they have remained in their infancy, and none of them has ever approached perfection, they all being at the present time the same as they were two or three thousand years ago.

The well-wishers to the cause of Christianity in Europe, who know nothing of the insuperable difficulties to be encountered every where in the dissemination of evangelical truths among the Hindoos of all castes, may indulge on this subject such speculations as they please, and such as their religious zeal may suggest to them. They may exclaim that "the Gospel is the true light that lighteth every man that cometh into the world;" that the truth, in its silent and slow, though steady march, must get the better of error, win the supercilious, soften the obdurate, fix the fickle, and overcome every obstacle that impedes its progress. Such pleasing dreams may be indulged within the precincts of a closet; but I would have those well-intentioned persons, who entertain them, to exercise my arduous profession only for a period of a few months, when I have no doubt they would become thoroughly convinced of the utter impossibility of carrying into effect their benevolent speculations among a people circumstanced as the Hindoos are.

That truth must open its way every where, and get the better of error and imposture, may be the case in ordinary circumstances, among persons whose reason and judgment are not perverted by unnatural passions and practices; among a people who silence their passions, and whose minds are open to argument and persuasion; or among persons disposed to know the truth, like the pious pagan Cornelius; "a devout man, and one that feared God with all his house, who gave much alms to the people, and prayed to God alway," (*Acts*, x.): but this, I fear, will never be the case with a people like the Hindoos, whose minds seem to be hermetically shut to the voice of truth, and to the rays of light; and whose judgment is led astray by their passions, and most of their public and private institutions. I have, alas! nowhere met, among the Hindoo Brahmins, another Cornelius, "whose prayers and alms are come up as a memorial before God." I have to this day remarked amongst them nothing but pride, self-conceit, duplicity, lying, and every kind of unnatural and anti-Christian vices.

The sun, by its brilliancy, dispels darkness, and irradiates the world, but it is only when its rays are not interrupted by any interposing cloud. Truth, in like manner, produces its effects, but it is only after men have silenced those passions and prejudices which impede its march.

Well-wishers to the cause of Christianity will say, "Are we then to be discouraged by difficulties, and altogether to desist from imparting to our Hindoo brethren the most valuable of divine favours—*Revelation?* and must we continue to see them immersed in the grossest idolatry without, at least, endeavouring to exhibit to their view the source and origin of the divine light? Shall we continue to be indifferent and cold spectators of the infamous worship of the Lingam? Shall we continue to behold, with apparent indifference, the prostitutions practised at Teroopatty in honour of *Vengattassuara*, the sacrifices of human victims often renewed in Orixa in the temple and in honour of *Jagnat*, and the frequent immolations of widows on the funeral pile of their deceased husbands; and must we continue to have our reason and understanding insulted by the serious recital of the most extravagant fables?

"You speak, Sir, in your letters, of the difficulties and contradictions to be met every where in India in the dissemination of evangelical truths; but were not the same difficulties met with in every nation where the Gospel has been preached? Did not Christ warn his followers that they should be hated, contradicted, and persecuted in every way, and in all manners? Did not the apostles and their successors disseminate the evangelical light amidst every kind of discouragement? Were they not 'buffeted, reviled, persecuted, and defamed?'. Were they not made 'a spectacle unto the world, and to angels, and to men?' Were they not made 'as the filth of the earth, and the offscouring of all things?' Was it not amidst all kinds of disadvantages that they preached the Gospel with such amazing success to kings and people, to the learned and the ignorant, to the barbarian and the polished; and laid the unshaken foundation of that faith of which Christ himself is the corner-stone, against which 'the gates of hell shall not prevail, and which shall last to the end of the world?'

"You speak of the Hindoos as an ignorant and unreflecting people; but is not the Christian religion that of the wise and the unwise, of the Greek and the barbarian? and is not its simple doctrines within the reach of the meanest capacity? On the other hand, does not christianity accommodate itself to all characters, and civil institutions? Has not its divine Author, by commanding men to 'render unto Cæsar what is Cæsar's,' accommodated it to every form of government? In short, is it worthy to be the religion of all climates, countries, and people?

"You mention the strong opposition to be met with on the part of an interested and crafty priesthood; but were cunning and craft peculiar to the priests of Seeva and Vishnoo?

Had not the first preachers of the Gospel the same difficulty to contend with in every pagan country? Did the priests of Mithra in Persia, of Osiris in Egypt, of Cérès and Cybele in Greece and Italy, the druids among the Celts, the priests of Odin in Scandinavia, &c. &c. yield their ground without strife and resistance? Did not the christian religion, without any other weapons than the Gospel, and without any other means but those of a mild persuasion, overcome every difficulty, and flourish amidst the severest persecutions? Did it not, within a short period, bring under its standard the polished Greece and the proud Italy? and was not the cross planted on the ruins of the Areopagus, and on the very summit of the capitol? Did it not bring under its laws the swarms of barbarians who, during many centuries, invaded and desolated the *lower empire?* and did not the ferocious Vandals finish by bending their necks under the yoke of the Gospel? Did not this holy religion overturn and supplant the druidical worship prevailing among the Cantabrians, the Gauls, the Britons, and the Germans, and establish itself among the fierce Scandinavians, on the ruins of the worship of Odin, and push its spiritual conquests to the polar circle, and the extremities of the world?

"Has it not had nearly similar success in modern times among pagan nations, to whom it was announced for the first time? Had it not the effect of civilizing, and bringing to habits of industry, the numerous hordes of savages who formerly wandered, with wild beasts, on the vast plains of Paragay? and was it not, at the beginning of the 17th century, on the point of altogether supplanting the worship of the Bowzes in Japan, and becoming there the national religion on the ruins of that of *Xaca* and *Amyda?* In short, was not the Gospel, in every country where it was preached, a bright light, which altogether dispelled the deep darkness of idolatry, of error, and imposture, to make shine in its place the truth in all its splendor and purity; as a shining sun whose bright beams pierce through the thickest mist, dissipate it, and purge the atmosphere of its noxious vapours?

"Why, then, should we despair of imparting to our Hindoo brethren the greatest of all benefits, and lay aside the design of rendering them happy both in this life, and in that to come? and why should this be the only nation on earth which should oppose insuperable obstacles to the introduction of the true religion among them, and among whom the word of God should fail of producing its effects; now chiefly when our holy religion is sheltered from open and direct persecution, and is enjoying a full toleration under the auspices of an enlightened and liberal government?"

So, no doubt, will the well-wishers to the cause of Christianity reason in Europe, and on those, or similar arguments, will they ground their benevolent hopes of the success of Christianity in India.

To all these speculations, I will briefly and in general answer, that in no country in the world has the Christian religion had to encounter the stupendous obstacles that are to be met with in India. In no country was the struggle so desperate; in none had it to deal with a people so completely priest-ridden; in none had it to oppose a system of cunning and priestcraft so deep laid, and so well calculated to baffle all the attempts of that divine religion to gain a solid footing; but, above all, in no country had it to encounter any difficulty resembling that baneful division of the people into castes which (whatever may be its advantages in other respects) has always proved, and will ever prove, an insurmountable bar to its progress. In consequence of this fatal division, nowhere but in India is a father reduced to the cruel and unnatural necessity of separating himself for ever from a beloved son who happens to embrace this religion; or a son to renounce for ever a tender father for the same reason. Nowhere is a spouse enjoined to divorce, for the same cause, a cherished husband; or an unmarried young person, after having embraced Christianity, doomed to pass the rest of his life in a forced state of celibacy. In no other country is a person who becomes a Christian exposed, by doing so, to the loss of kindred, friends, goods, possessions, and all that he holds dear. In no country, in short, is a man, by becoming a convert to Christianity, cast out as a vagrant from society, proscribed and shunned by all: and yet all this happens in India, and a Hindoo who turns Christian must submit himself to all these, and many other no less severe trials.

Let us also consider the wide difference which exists, in many other respects, between the Hindoos and the other nations of the world, and let this consideration teach us not to be misled in this matter by precedents, or by arguments *à pari*, or *à fortiori*.

Among other nations, both ancient and modern, civilized and savage, there always existed a chain of communication, which taught them that each of them formed only a part of the great body of society, and that they stood in want of each other. They, in general, were disposed to profit by the improvement of each other; and although their priests and religious leaders had generally engrossed the whole of the mysteries of religion, and of religious knowledge, which they were careful not to communicate injudiciously to the vulgar, yet the other individuals were allowed to judge for themselves in profane matters, or at least in their private and domestic concerns. They were, moreover, allowed philosophical and many other pursuits, which gave them ample room to exert their intellectual faculties. They were fond of new discoveries, and their minds were open to argument, reasoning, and persuasion.

The Hindoo, on the contrary, has been bereft of his reason and understanding by his crafty religious guides; he cannot (as has been already observed) in any circumstance judge for himself, not even in his domestic concerns, or the most trifling occurrences of life. All is invariably ruled by his unchangeable institutions. Imparting or receiving knowledge is a crime, and listening for the purpose to any other but his religious leaders, the Brahmins, is considered as a heinous transgression.

An Hindoo, and above all, a Brahmin, by his institutions, his usages, his education and customs, must be considered as a kind of moral monster, as an individual placed in a state of continual variance and opposition with the rest of the human race; as a being sequestrated from mankind, with whom he is forbidden all free and confidential intercourse, nay, whom he is obliged to shun, to scorn, and to hate. The crafty Brahmins, (in order that the system of imposture that establishes their unmolested superiority over the other tribes, and brings the latter under their uncontroled bondage, might in no way be discovered or questioned,) had the foresight to draw up between the Hindoos and the other nations on earth an impassable, an impregnable line, that defies all attacks from foreigners. There is no opening to approach them, and they themselves are strictly, and under the severest penalties, precluded from access to any body for the purpose of improving themselves, and bettering their actual condition, than which, as they are firmly and universally persuaded, nothing on the earth is more perfect.

On the other hand, it will be acknowledged, I believe, by every unbiassed observer, that as long as we are unable to make impression on the polished part of the nation, on the leaders of public opinion, on the body of Brahmins in short, there remain but very faint hopes of propagating Christianity among the Hindoos; and as long as the only result of our labours shall be, as is at present the case, to bring into our respective communions here and there a few desperate vagrants, outcasts, pariahs, horse-keepers, beggars, and other persons of the lowest description, the impression made on the public mind cannot fail to be unfavourable, and detrimental to the interests of Christianity among a people who, in all circumstances, are ruled by the force of custom and example, and are in no case allowed to judge for themselves.

Now, there is no possibility to have access, either by word or writing, to the refined part of the nation; the line of separation between us and the brahmins is (as I have just observed) drawn, and the barrier impassable; there is no opening to argument or persuasion: our opponents are strictly bound by their religious and civil statutes to shun, to scorn, and hate us. They are obliged to do so from a sense of duty. To listen to us would be in them a crime, and the greatest of all disgraces.

I have already given an imperfect description of the Hindoo Brahmin by representing him as a kind of moral monster in the social order; as a being whose institutions are generally a deviation from the order of nature, and who has nothing to do with the rest of mankind, from whom he has entirely insulated himself.

The leading feature of the education of a Christian, is an universal charity and benevolence towards all his fellow-creatures.

The leading feature of the education of a Brahmin is an universal hatred and contempt towards all the human race.

A Christian is taught to love even his enemies, and to return good for evil.

A Brahmin is taught, if not positively to hate his friends, and to return evil for good, at least to conduct himself through life by quite selfish considerations, and to sacrifice all, without exception, to his private interests, without distinction between friends and foes; to be entirely unmindful of the services rendered to him, and to consider them, whatever may be their importance and value, as his strict due.

A Brahmin is, moreover, obliged from duty to be selfish, intolerant and proud, insolent and forbidding. He is brought up in the indelible idea that he is the only perfect being on earth, a being of by far a superior stamp to that of all other mortals; that all other men are nothing but barbarians; that he owes nothing to any body; and that all his fellow-creatures are created to live under his bondage. Now, I ask every reasonable man whether, so long as we have to oppose a body professing such principles, we can flatter ourselves with the hope of making the slightest impression on a people living under their absolute control?

The more I consider the principles and conduct of those leaders of the public opinion in India, the more I become persuaded that there is something preternatural in this caste of Hindoos; I am the more appalled and confounded by the subject, and I cannot account for it otherwise but by supposing that on account of their quite unnatural habits, they are lying under the divine wrath and curse. I cannot help looking upon them as upon those false philosophers of whom Paul speaks (*Rom.* i.), "who, professing themselves wise, are become fools;" whom, for having perverted their own reason, and that of others, "God gave over to a reprobate mind.... and to the lust of their own heart," &c. &c.

In common with those philosophers mentioned by St. Paul, the Brahmins entertain, respecting the only true God, and his divine attributes, as clear and pure ideas as a people unassisted by the light of divine revelation can have; but to that Supreme Being they pay no worship whatever, and besides they make it a duty never to communicate to what they term the stupid vulgar this most important truth of the existence of only one God. "They hold the truth in unrighteousness.... so that they are without excuse, because that when they knew God, they glorified him not as God.... They changed the truth of God into a lie..... Wherefore the wrath of God is revealed from heaven against them, and God gave them up unto vile affections."

In reading this chapter of our holy books, and the forcible style in which the Apostle treats the subject, one would fancy that he had in view the Hindoo Brahmins when he wrote it. If one would draw up the character of this caste of Hindoos, it could not be better done than by literally transcribing the 29th, 30th, and 31st verses of this very chapter.

Such is the short sketch of the unexampled difficulties against which the Christian religion has to contend in India. I now leave it to every candid and unprejudiced observer, to every person the least acquainted with the nature of man, to decide whether, amidst such stupendous obstacles, there remains any opening for the truth making its way, and whether we may entertain the remotest hope of Christianity gaining ground among a people so circumstanced?

That God, in his infinite mercy, will have all men "to be saved, and to come to the knowledge of the truth;" and that Christ died for the salvation of all mankind, and "came into this world to save sinners;" are truths acknowledged by all sorts of Christians, if we except perhaps a few who maintain the gloomy tenet that God is willing to save only the elect, or predestined. It is at the same time no less certain that from hidden secrets in the divine councils, the knowledge of the truth has, from the origin of the world, been the happy lot of only the minority of mankind.

Not to speak of the antediluvian race, when all men had run headlong into the deepest abyss of idolatry, and "all flesh had corrupted his way upon the earth," with the exception of a single family which had kept unpolluted the true belief in God; after the deluge, and chiefly from the famous event which took place on the plains of *Shinnaar*, (the building of the tower of Babel,) to the vocation of Abraham, the truth, it appears, had again disappeared from the earth, or the knowledge of the true God was confined to a very small number of holy personages, who preserved inviolate this sacred deposit. This, the most important of all truths, began to be more generally and better known under the patriarchs; and was promulgated in a solemn and indelible manner under the Mosaical law. Although the chosen people frequently apostatised from the only true religion, yet they were brought back to the paths of righteousness by the divine interposition, or by the unremitted admonitions of the prophets and other just men who lived among them, and who, amidst the general defection, stood steadfastly attached to the true worship; yet at those times, and to the very coming of the Messiah, the revealed religion made no sensible progress. The truth was known but to very small numbers, and it may be said that, in those early days, this world, which God had created as a manifestation of his omnipotence, had been converted into a vast temple of idols, since the knowledge of the true God was confined to a small corner of the world, and the Lord had only worshippers in the temple of Jerusalem.

After the coming of Christ, the true religion was promulgated all over the world, and had such extraordinary successes amidst every kind of discouragement and contradiction; that it is quite impossible to account for it but by the supernatural and invisible interference and assistance of the divine agent, who alone was able to overcome the otherwise insuperable obstacles that opposed its progress, and to extend its empire over so large a proportion of mankind. We are obliged, however, to confess, that notwithstanding its early amazing progress, the revealed religion has to this day been that of only the minority of mankind; and that if we except the spiritual conquest it has made in modern times in the new world, and in the Philippine Islands, in which alone the Spaniards are said to have gained over to Christianity about two millions of natives, it has, from a period of about a thousand years, remained stationary in the old, making no sensible progress among the heathen nations during so long a period, and rather losing than gaining ground. Its conquests in Asia, from the epoch of the Portuguese invasion to this day, are rather insignificant, and I apprehend that I am rather over-rating the number of the converts made in this part of the world, by stating them to be twelve hundred thousand; nearly half of this number may be found in the peninsula of

India and the island of Ceylon, and the rest in the kingdoms of Pegu, Siam, Laos, Cambodje, Cochin-china, Tunkin, and in China, in which countries missionaries have been sent, almost without intermission, during the last two or three centuries. Now this number, scattered among a population of perhaps more than five hundred millions of inhabitants, will appear very inconsiderable indeed, and very far from compensating for the heavy losses the true religion has sustained in several other countries, from Mahometan invasions, and other causes.

Now, who has told us that Christianity shall not remain stationary in like manner, and continue to the end of the world to be the religion of only the minority of mankind. Christ (as I mentioned in another letter) has, it is true, promised that " the Gospel of the kingdom shall be published in all the world, for a witness unto all nations, and then shall the end come." His sacred pledge, in this respect, has been fulfilled, or is still fulfilling, but, at the same time, has he told any one that all nations, or even the majority of them, should be brought under the yoke of the Gospel?

It is true, that in several of the books of the Old Testament, and chiefly in the Psalms of David, in which frequent allusions to the coming of the Messiah are made, he is represented as extending his spiritual dominion over all the earth, from one end of the world to the other; but most of the expressions used by the inspired writers in those passages of Holy Writ either have a mystical meaning, or are mere metaphors which cannot be taken in their literal import, and whose true meaning cannot be perfectly understood by us.

The ways of God, in his gratuitous election of only a part of his creatures, are to us (as I observed in a former letter) an unfathomable mystery, a hidden secret, which may never be revealed to us in this life; for "who hath known the mind of the Lord, or who hath been his counsellor?" Whenever I reflect upon this awful subject, my weak understanding is quite confounded at the apparent darkness that surrounds it; and, like St. Paul, I stop my wandering thoughts, and fix my irresolute mind, by humbly exclaiming, with him, "O the depth of the riches, both of the wisdom and knowledge of God! How just are his judgments, and his ways past finding out!"

"Many widows (says Christ, in allusion to this mysterious subject,) were in Israel in the days of Elias, when the heaven was shut up three years and six months, when general famine was throughout all the land, but unto none of them was Elias sent, save unto Sarepta, a city of Sidon, unto a woman that was a widow; and many lepers were in Israel in the time of Elijeus the prophet, and none of them was cleansed, saving Naaman the Syrian." (Luke, iv. 25, 26, 27.)

Faith, and other supernatural virtues, are merely a gratuitous gift from God, which he bestows on whom he pleases, when he pleases, and on what conditions he pleases. He may, therefore, without even an appearance of injustice, require as a condition from those to whom the boon is tendered, that they shall throw no unnatural obstacles into his way; that they shall not pervert the use of their reason by unnatural passions; that they shall not run into extravagancies which reason loudly reprobates, and against which all nature bears testimony; and that they shall not allow themselves to be misled by a religious worship, the folly of which heaven and earth loudly and openly proclaim. But still more, the dispositions of God, and above all, his hidden system of election and reprobation, are quite out of the reach of our weak understanding.

From the beginning of the world, the true religion has journeyed from one country to another. It has passed from one people to another; it has been in several instances taken away from one nation, and transferred to another: several people who had been enlightened by the light of Revelation fell into the darkness of idolatry or Mahometanism. While, on the other hand, " the people who sat in darkness saw great light, and to them which sat in the region and shadow of death, light sprung up." "Qui non viderant, viderunt, et qui viderant cæci facti sunt." (John, ix.) Amidst all these changes of abode, amidst the revolutions which occasioned them, the true faith continued unstained, and received no blemish, no more, indeed, than does the bright and glowing sun, when, leaving one hemisphere in darkness, he passes to the other to irradiate it with all his splendor.

We have seen in ancient and modern times Christian and heathen nations, which, having filled up the measure of their iniquities, and gone far beyond the limits of divine forbearance, have been cursed, reprobated, and finally exterminated under the divine wrath. We have striking examples of this in our sacred records: nothing short of the utter extermination of the wicked nations which peopled the land of Canaan was able to satisfy divine justice. All the worshippers of Moloch and Belphegor were under the same anathema, and all that profligate race were doomed to a general and total destruction.

Are the worshippers of the Lingam less culpable than those of Belphegor? and is the worship of Jagnot and Teroopatty less nefarious than than of Moloch? Are we not warranted, on beholding the unnatural and odious worship which prevails all over India, in thinking that these unhappy people are lying under an everlasting anathema; that by obstinately refusing to listen to the voice of the heavens, which "declare the glory of God," they have for ever rendered themselves unworthy of the divine favours; that by obstinately rejecting the word of God, which has been in vain announced to them without intermission, during these last three or four centuries, they have "filled up the measure of their fathers," have been entirely forsaken by God, and (what is the worst of divine vengeance) given over for ever to a reprobate mind, on account of the peculiar wickedness of their worship, which supposes, in those among whom it prevails, a degree of perversity far beyond that of all old Pagan nations?

In fact, the inferiority of the Hindoo Brahmins to all other Pagan nations, with respect to religion, is the more striking, as they have not been able to distinguish what is a virtue, and what is not, since they in general suppose it much more meritorious to render service to beasts than to men. A pious Hindoo Brahmin, who will make it his imperative duty to share his frugal meal with fishes, snakes, monkeys, and birds of prey, will, on the other hand, behold, with the coldest indifference, a poor wretch starving at his door, without thinking of assisting him.

Instead of that great leading precept of Christian charity, "Thou shalt love thy neighbour like thyself," which is calculated to convert the whole of mankind into a community of brothers, it might be said that the leading precept of the Brahmins is this, "Thou shalt love brutes like thyself."

It is true that the Hindoos, in general, are by no means strangers to most of the moral and social virtues which are innate in our natures, and common to all civilised people; but they have been unable to apply those virtues to their proper objects, or when applied to suitable objects, they have robbed them of their intrinsical merits by the most selfish motives, or the most childish vanity. To practise a virtue from quite disinterested motives, and only to enjoy the inward satisfaction of doing good, are things above their comprehension. Ask a rich Hindoo who spends the whole or a part of his fortune in erecting or repairing places of religious worship, in building choulteries, as a shelter for the weary traveller, or in lining public roads with trees, to refresh them by their shade; in digging wells and tanks for the benefit of the public, and in such like charitable undertakings; what are his motives for so doing, his answer will almost invariably be, that he does so to be publicly praised as a virtuous man during his life, and to transmit his name to posterity after his death.

Let it not be supposed that I indulge in this strain of speech to abuse or revile the unhappy Hindoos; far be from me even the naked thought of insulting them on the score of their errors in religious or other matters, how monstrous soever they may appear to me. Their blindness and obstinacy on this subject have at all times excited in my mind only feelings of compassion at their misfortunes. In beholding the extravagance of their idolatrous worship, I cannot help exclaiming with the prophet king, and with the liveliest sense of gratitude to Heaven; "Beatus homo quem tu erudieris Domine, et de lege tua docueris eum." And when I behold them prostrating themselves before their gods of stone and brass, I exclaim, "Such were our ancestors, and so did they, and so would we ourselves do, had not God, through his infinite mercy, taken us out of such an abyss of darkness, in order to illumine us with the bright light of his divine Revelation! Let everlasting thanks be returned to Him, for this the greatest of all his divine favors in this life."

But it will be said, will the actual extensive intercourse of the natives with the Europeans be of no avail to the former with respect to their religious improvement; will it not at least excite in their minds a spirit of enquiry, and a desire to know the truth; dispel by little and little the thick clouds of ignorance that hang over them, and bring them back to sounder notions on religion?

I cannot refrain from smiling at the idea that the conduct and examples of the existing race of Europeans of any nation whatever, will be able to bring the Hindoos to just notions on this subject, and instil into their minds principles of morality and religion. The reverse has to this day been the case, and (as I stated in a former letter) it is most certain that the intercourse of the Hindoos with the Europeans has proved the last blow to the interests of Christianity in India, and that the repeated invasions of the country by the latter, have put a stop to all further conversion, and only contributed to make apostates among the old converts, by rendering them objects of universal contempt among all classes of Hindoos.

It is, I believe, generally admitted, that the invasions and conquests which the Europeans, prompted by avarice and an unextinguishable thirst of dominion, have not ceased to make in the old and new world during the last three or four centuries, have, in most cases, proved rather a curse than a blessing, and have, on the whole, produced more evil than good. Not to speak of the flood of blood through which those conquests were made, and the European dominions established, the invaders, among many other evils, have supplied the savages with fermented poisonous liquors, with the use of which they were formerly unacquainted, and which have increased their natural ferocity to a considerable extent.

They are become the general carriers, and almost the exclusive monopolists of that poisonous drug called opium, whose effects are to produce complete madness; and from an insatiable thirst for gain, they have shamelessly smuggled that poison all over Asia, in open violation of the wise prohibitions of the rulers of several countries to prevent so pernicious an article from being introduced into the states under their sway. They have had the horrid distinction of teaching the half-civilized people their infernal system of warfare, and supplied them with the most destructive kind of weapons, the more effectually to destroy each other. They have, in general, by their bad examples, polluted their minds, and vitiated the simplicity of their manners. They have poisoned their bodies by loathsome and incurable diseases, till then unknown to them; but, perhaps, with a few exceptions, they have to this day operated no material improvement in their morals or religion; on which points, the conquered are found to be, at present, rather in a worse condition than they were when their fierce invaders, stepping over the immense barriers by which nature seemed to have separated them for ever, and violating their territories and their natural rights, made their first appearance among them.

During the long period I have been in India, I have visited places inhabited by Europeans of several nations, by English, French, Dutch, Danes, and Portuguese. In none of those places have I been able to remark any amelioration or improvement in the morals and religion of the natives. Any changes I have observed in this respect, were rather for the worse. If their intercourse with the Europeans has operated any alteration, it has been to prompt them to lay aside and disregard all that was good and justifiable in their usages, retaining all that is bad and exceptionable.

Nobody can deny that the Hindoos have to this day copied nothing of the Europeans besides their vices and their follies. They have been at all times but too well disposed to imitate their bad examples, whilst, on the other hand, their virtues, the spirit of charity, of liberality, of compassion and benevolence, which characterise most Europeans, have not even been noticed by the Hindoos in general.

This circumstance may be distinctly noticed by every observer, who travels over the country. Let him go to the coast, or any other place inhabited by Europeans, he will find there the natives in general, selfish, arrogant, impertinent, impatient of control, obtrusive, insolent towards Europeans, ever ready to injure or insult them, when they think they may do so with impunity. Let him call for any purpose in those parts of the country on any native who in speaking to him lies under no restraint, or is not overawed by interested considerations, and who thinks that he may without danger to himself deal freely with him, he will easily remark in his words and his countenance how very conscious he is of his high superiority over him. He will observe in his forbidding looks, or in his affected sneer, the expression of the inward contempt he entertains towards him, as forcibly as if he said openly in his face, "I am a civilised man, and thou art a barbarian; I am in my country, and thou art a foreigner; I am in my place, and thou art an obtruder; if thou art my superior in physical force, I am thine in education and every kind of intellectual endowments."

Let the same person go into the inland country, or into places where the Europeans are not at all, or but little known, and he will in general find a people, shy it is true, but docile, peaceable, unassuming, submissive, serviceable, respectful to Europeans, and ready to render them service, whenever the latter betray nothing forbidding in their manners and behaviour.

So far from the intercourse of the Europeans with the natives making a favourable impression on the latter, on the score of religion, this very circumstance produces (as I mentioned in a former letter) a quite opposite effect.

On the whole, it is my decided opinion, that as long as we have no warmer promoters of the cause of Christianity than the existing race of Europeans of any nation whatever, we can entertain but very faint hopes of Christianity gaining ground in India. As long as a native Christian, who happens to fall in the way of an European, shall (after having been surveyed with a stern and scornful countenance) be welcomed by him with this insulting reproach, "Why hast thou forsaken the religion of thy forefathers to embrace a foreign worship?" so long as the name of a native Christian and a rogue shall sound as synonymous in the ears of a prejudiced European; so long as the deluded victims who devote themselves to the most arduous of all professions, forego all worldly prospects in life, and sacrifice their repose, their health, and their lives, for the purpose of imparting to their fellow-creatures (what they consider as the most valuable of all blessings,) the knowledge of the only one true God, and of the worship due to him by all his creatures, shall be branded with the appellation of fanatics, idiots, and other the like opprobrious epithets; so long as the Hindoos shall hear the Europeans themselves, making in several instances their own religion, and its sacred records, the subject of their paltry sarcasms and railleries; so long as the natives shall behold the precepts and morals of that holy religion openly violated without shame or scruple by those who were educated in its bosom; in short, so long as the Christian religion shall have to struggle with so many domestic and foreign obstacles, it would, in my humble opinion, be perfect nonsense to flatter ourselves with the hope of its ever gaining any solid footing in the country.

I will now say a few words on the project of enlightening the Hindoos, by the translation of the Holy Scriptures, and their circulation among them. But as I have already treated this subject in a former letter, what I have to add shall be confined to a few short remarks.

It appears to me, that we are a little too much disposed to over-rate the effects that we fancy the naked divine work ought to produce on the mind of an ill-disposed heathen nation. We judge of the effects it ought to produce on them, by those it produces on ourselves, who have been brought under its instructions; who received it in our early years from Christian parents; and who have perhaps made it our principal study in our maturer age.

To start in the work of proselytism by exhibiting at once to the view of the pagans of any nation whatever our holy books, is in my opinion to commence our labours where we ought to finish them; it is to build an edifice before having laid its foundations; it is the same as to require from an apprentice in mechanics to form a complicated machine, without supplying him with tools for the purpose; it is worse, it is to call upon a man, just come out of the hands of nature, upon a savage, whom we would wish to make a perfect mechanic, and to whom, after showing a model composed of a great number of complicated wheels and springs, we should say, "Here is your model; learn your trade from it: when you have succeeded to imitate it, we will receive you into the profession of a mechanic. We say nothing more to you on the subject. Take the model in your hand, and shift for yourself; commence by finding out iron mines, extract the iron from the ore, make your axes, your saw, and other tools, fell your trees, work your timber, your wheels, and your springs, and finish your machine." Would not the savage, on hearing such language, be disposed to think that his master intended to make a jest of him? or if he believed that he spoke seriously, would he not be appalled at the task imposed on him, and in his despair would he not break in pieces the model left in his hand, and fly again to his forest and native wilds?

We have many instances of Christians accustomed to read and interpret the Holy Scriptures, passing from one sect to another, and endeavouring to justify this change by the meaning, or the liberal interpretation of the word of God; but I have never heard of a single instance of a pagan having been converted to any sect of Christianity by the simple reading of the naked text of our sacred books. This is certainly the primitive source from which our faith is derived, and the foundation on which it is built; but it is so far above the comprehension of our unprepared understanding, that it would be unreasonable on our part to expect an uncultivated and unassisted mind to be able to decide for itself, and to build his faith on it alone.

Our holy records afford us a striking instance of the insufficiency of this means alone to build up one's faith in the example of the Eunuch of Candace, (*Acts* viii.) who probably was not a man of common parts or education.

He was returning from Jerusalem, and, sitting in his chariot, was reading on his way Esaias the prophet. Philip, warned by an angel, passed on the same road, and prompted by the spirit, he ran to him, and heard him read the prophet Esaias, and said, "Understandest thou what thou readest?" Hear now the candid answer of the Eunuch: "And he said, How can I (understand it), except some man should guide me? And he desired that he would come up, and sit with him," &c. &c. "Then Philip opened his mouth, and preached unto him Jesus," &c. (See the whole of this edifying occurrence in the quoted chapter.)

Far be from me the thought of failing in the least in profound respect and veneration for the sacred word of God, or of detracting a single particle from the salutary effects it is calculated to produce on a well-disposed person, who makes it his study, with the intention of becoming acquainted with his duties as a man and Christian. But I repeat it, to exhibit the Scriptures to an unprepared pagan, to build up his faith upon them, or even to excite in his mind a spirit of enquiry or a desire to know the truth, is, in my humble opinion, an absurd proceeding.

I believe that I may without presumption, assert the same with respect to the native

Christians in general. I have now under my religious control between 7000 and 8000 persons of this description; and I should be very much perplexed indeed, were I among so large a number desired to point out four individuals capable of understanding the meaning of the Bible, and to whom the reading of the naked text of the Holy Scriptures would prove of the least utility.

I have composed for the instruction of this my large flock, a short catechism comprised within ten or twelve pages, explanatory of the principal truths of the Christian religion. This small composition is worded in the simplest and plainest manner, and to make it better understood, I have also repeatedly explained it in various ways to my congregations; yet I find that after so much trouble, the great majority of them do not understand it. Now, I beg leave to ask of any candid and unprejudiced person, of what utility can the Holy Scriptures be to persons unable to understand a short catechism of ten pages, composed in the plainest style?

Nobody is better persuaded than myself of the quite disinterested intentions of the Bible Society. I feel that it would be extremely impertinent in me to make insinuations in the least offensive to that learned body; but I cannot help saying that their endeavours to enlighten the Hindoos, or to make the least impression on them through the translation of the Holy Scriptures circulated among them, are, in my opinion, quite lost trouble, and will be of no avail. I cannot moreover help declaring, that the money spent for the purpose would be better and more meritoriously employed in feeding the hungry and clothing the naked.

It is of no utility to distribute Bibles if you have not well-founded hopes that they will be read, and their meaning be understood. Now, I have every reason to apprehend, that as long as they shall be translated into the almost unintelligible style in which we see the versions already executed, there is not the remotest hope of their being of the least utility even to the best disposed persons, and that (as I observed in a foregoing letter) those loose and spurious versions will only tend to increase the contempt of the prejudiced natives against Christianity, and prove on the whole detrimental to its interests.

In fact, if one of the many proofs of our holy books being of divine origin be derived from their intrinsic worth, from their noble, inimitable, and majestic simplicity, there is, alas! on the other hand, but too much room to fear that the Hindoos will form a directly opposite judgment on the subject, when they behold the quite ludicrous and vulgar style of the versions at present circulated among them; and that even the most reasonable and best disposed, on perusing the Scriptures under such a contemptible shape, so far from looking upon them as the work of God, will, on the contrary, be strongly impelled to consider them as mere forgeries of some obscure, ignorant, and illiterate individual, and of course as a downright imposture.

Among many instances which are come within my personal notice of the effects produced on the minds of the natives by the versions of the Holy Scriptures into the idioms of India, I will content myself with relating the following only: —

Being in a neighbouring village, three or four months ago, I received there the visit of some Christians living in the *Bellary* district, in a place called *Talairu*, where between 30 and 40 *Tilinga* Christian families reside. After the ordinary marks of respect, and the usual compliments, one of my visitors took a book out of a small bag, and without uttering a single word, laid it at my feet. On opening it, I found it was a translation into *Tilinga* of the Gospel of St. Matthew; and before saying any thing about it, I wished to be acquainted with the opinion of my visitors on the work. Having interrogated them for the purpose, the person who had delivered it to me began the following curious account, saying that some months back two Christians of their village went to Bellary on some business, and hearing that a European *gooroo*, or priest, (whom from their account I understood to have been a protestant missionary,) was living in that place, they went to pay him a visit; that they had been very kindly received by him, and that after a good deal of conversation, chiefly on religious subjects, the gooroo, on dismissing them, had made them a present of the book, strongly recommending them to have a chapter of its contents read every Sunday in their chapel to the assembled congregation; that there being only five or six individuals among the congregation who could write and read, on their return they had called on them, and delivered the book to them; that these persons had assembled together for the purpose of reading it, and becoming acquainted with its contents; but that they were unable to understand the meaning of a single chapter; that in their perplexity they had applied to some pagans living in the same village, to assist them in expounding the book; but no one among them had been able to understand any thing about it; that they were then disposed to believe that the foreign *gooroo*, who was not their own, had given them such a work to make a jest of them, and that in this persuasion, some were of opinion, that it should be thrown into the fire; but the majority wishing to become acquainted at least with the outlines of the work, called for the purpose on a brahmin *poorohita*, or astrologer, living in their neighbourhood (which circumstance of Christians having recourse to a pagan astrologer, to expound the gospel to them, is not the least curious); that the poorohita having perused one or two pages in their presence, told them that it appeared to him to be a curious book, but that it was written in so loose and incoherent a style, and in so obscure a manner, that it would require some days to become acquainted with the whole. He therefore dismissed them, telling them to come back after a few days.

When the Christians returned, the poorohita gave them the following curious answer, assuring them, in a low tone of voice, that he had thoroughly perused the work with attention, and that it was nothing more or less than a treatise upon *magic*; adding, that it was worked up in obscure and incoherent sentences, quite unintelligible to *sudras;* "as is always the case," said he, "with works treating upon occult and pernicious sciences;" and strongly recommending them to destroy, or otherwise get rid of it, as it was a great sin to keep so pernicious a book in their possession.

Such is the account those poor simple fellows gave me of the gospel of St. Matthew. The fact is, that the *poorohita* himself had been unable to understand any thing about it; but as he was unwilling to confess his ignorance before *sudras,* he thought he had better give them this awkward explanation. This anecdote will give you some idea of the versions of the Holy Scriptures now extant in the country, and of their utility.

In fact, it was not in that way that the first missionaries, who made their appearance in the country more than three hundred years ago, gained some ground, and got a hearing. It was not by circulating amongst the natives spurious, and almost unintelligible versions of our sacred book, that they made some impression in those early times; it was chiefly by scrupulously conforming themselves to the usages and customs of the country; it was by becoming Hindoos in their habits and manner of living, that they insinuated themselves amongst these people. In the meanwhile, as, notwithstanding the precautions they employed to obtain a free and quite unrestrained intercourse with the natives, their colour, their being foreigners, and other circumstances, excited distrust; in order to remove this obstacle to their successes, they had recourse to the following means: —

After having made a certain number of proselytes, they selected the best-disposed, and most intelligent among them, and established schools for the forming of catechists, or native religious teachers. The missionaries superintended and directed those schools of catechists, and made it their principal study to give them an education suited to their intended profession. They, in consequence, composed several religious tracts explanatory of the Creed and of the Ten Commandments; whilst other tracts were also written containing some plain and short proofs of the existence of the only true God, an explanation of his divine attributes, and a refutation of the idolatry prevailing in the country. After the catechists had properly become acquainted with these matters, they were taken into the service of the missionaries, and taught the manner of introducing themselves by good manners among the natives.

These native catechists introduced themselves easily every where; into the markets and other places of public resort; into private houses and elsewhere; as physicians, merchants, and under other denominations, without exciting any distrust. In their free intercourse with the world, they were taught by their employers dexterously to provoke discussion upon religion; and so to manage such disputes, as that in making a display of their own learning they should in no way excite suspicion. When they perceived that they were listened to without disapprobation, they returned, and continued their discussions, without any pretensions to superior information. When they saw that they had made an impression on any one of their hearers, they prevailed upon him to accompany them to the missionary, who finished the work.

Such was the manner of proceeding of the first missionaries, and the way by which they gained some ground in this country in better times. Those schools for forming good catechists were the only ones established by the missionaries, and under their immediate superintendence. They continued, without interruption, to a late period, and were finally suppressed about fifty years ago; nearly at the period when the European invasions taking place rendered (as I have remarked in another letter) the Christian religion an object of universal opprobrium all over the country; and no means whatever remained of getting from the pagans a further hearing on the subject, either through native catechists or otherwise.

Warned by long experience, I repeat it, with feelings of the deepest sorrow, that there remain, in the present circumstances, no human means of improving Christian knowledge among the natives of India. The concerns of the Christian religion are in a quite desperate state; from a long period, all missionaries who are come to India for the purpose of making proselytes, have found themselves deceived on their arrival in the country, have experienced nothing but the most distressing disappointments in all their pursuits, and all their labours have terminated in nothing.

For my part, I cannot boast of my successes in this holy career during a period of twenty-five years that I have laboured to promote the interests of the Christian religion. The restraints and privations under which I have lived, by conforming myself to the usages of the country; embracing, in many respects, the prejudices of the natives; living like them, and becoming almost a Hindoo myself; in short, by "being made all things to all men, that I might by all means save some,"—all this has proved of no avail to me to make proselytes.

During the long period I have lived in India, in the capacity of a missionary, I have made, with the assistance of a native missionary, in all between two and three hundred converts of both sexes. Of this number two-thirds were pariahs, or beggars; and the rest were composed of *sudras*, vagrants, and outcasts of several tribes, who, being without resource, turned Christians, in order to form new connections, chiefly for the purpose of marriage, or with some other interested views. Among them are to be found some also who believed themselves to be possessed by the devil, and who turned Christians, after having been assured that on their receiving baptism the unclean spirits would leave them, never to return; and I will declare it, with shame and confusion, that I do not remember any one who may be said to have embraced Christianity from conviction, and through quite disinterested motives. Among these new converts many apostatised, and relapsed into Paganism, finding that the Christian religion did not afford them the temporal advantages they had looked for in embracing it; and I am verily ashamed, that the resolution I have taken to declare the whole truth on this subject forces me to make the humiliating avowal, that those who continued Christians are the very worst among my flock.

I know that my brother-missionaries in other parts of the country, although more active, and more zealous, perhaps, than myself, have not been more fortunate, either in the number or the quality of their proselytes. For my part, I have, until now, struggled, though in vain, with the numberless difficulties stated in these letters, and exerted myself to the utmost not to sink under so many disadvantages. If a great many persons of my profession have discharged their duties with more ability, I believe that I may boast that few have done it with more patience and perseverance than myself; and in spite of every kind of disgust and contradiction, in spite of the inutility of my pursuits, I am determined, after having embraced the profession of a missionary, to continue the desperate struggle, and persevere in it to the last.

In fact, the conversion of the Hindoos, under existing circumstances, is so hopeless a thing, and their prejudices against it are so deeply rooted, and so decidedly declared, that I am firmly persuaded, that if (what has never been the case) the Hindoo Brahmins were animated by a spirit of proselytism, and sent to

Europe missionaries of their own faith, to propagate their monstrous religion, and make converts to the worship of Seeva and Vishnoo, they would have much more chance of success, among certain classes of society, than we have to make among them true converts to the faith in Christ.

But, to conclude, let the beholding of the monstrous worship which prevails all over India — let the blindness and hardness of heart of a people immersed in such an abyss of darkness, be a warning to those who have the happiness of being born under a religion which gives them such sound, and such pure notions of the Divinity. The spectacle of whole nations still immersed in the most extravagant and obstinate idolatry, forcibly apprises us of the total incapacity of unassisted human reason, to make to itself a reasonable system of religion, and of the necessity of a foreign divine light, to guide us aright in this important path; it reminds us, also, of the great obligations under which we stand to the divine Author of revelation, the common Father of all mankind, for having, without any previous deserving on our part, chosen us, among so many idolatrous nations, to be his adopted people. What ought not our gratitude to be to him for this, the greatest of all his divine favours?

Many persons who come from Europe to India, with unsettled and wavering religious principles, finish, on beholding the variety of worships prevailing in the country, by laying aside what they term the prejudices of education, becoming free-thinkers, and adopting the broad principle of modern philosophy, that all religions are equally acceptable to the Deity, and conduct to the same end.

For my part, I rejoice that these fallacious notions have never been mine: I always viewed the subject in a quite different manner; and the sight of the monstrous worship prevailing in India, so far from staggering my faith, has, on the contrary, contributed in a high degree to strengthen it. In fact, whenever I compare the majestic simplicity of our Scriptures, the unspotted sanctity of our gospel, the impressive solemnity of our religious worship, with the heap of impertinent, absurd, and obscene tales contained in the pooranes and legends of the Hindoos, and with the extravagant, barbarous, and, in many instances, horrid worship of the country, the Christian religion alone appears to me stamped with the seal of divinity. In these circumstances I forcibly experience feelings of the liveliest gratitude for the blessing of being born under a religion, the only one on earth which gives us sound and pure notions of the Deity, his divine attributes, and the worship due to him by all reasonable creatures. Impressed with these feelings, I cannot help exclaiming with the holy legislator of the Hebrews, "What nation is there so great that hath statutes and judgments so righteous as all this law which I set before you this day." (Deut. iv. 8.)

I will say nothing about the leading feature of the printed report, a copy of which you sent me, relating to the improving of the condition of the unhappy offspring of the Europeans of the lower classes, left quite destitute and helpless in society, and exposed to every kind of danger, both spiritual and temporal. This important subject is so ably and so forcibly treated in the sermon you delivered on the occasion, that nothing more need be said about it. I observed, with the greatest gratification, that the sad condition of those unfortunate beings had at last attracted the attention it so well deserves, of sensible and benevolent persons; that much for their improvement had already been done, and much more was in contemplation. I hope, and sincerely wish, that your humane, generous, and religious endeavours, and those of your worthy associates in the cause of humanity, may be accompanied with success, and that the happiest results may follow from these your labours. It is a subject which had long called for the attention of sensible souls, preferably to any other charitable object; for it might be said with truth, morally and physically, of these helpless children, in the words of Jeremiah, "The young children ask bread, and no man breaketh it unto them."

I will now close the discussion I have carried on in this and the foregoing letters. When I commenced them, I did not imagine I should go so far into the question. I was induced to enter into so many details by the consideration that elucidations on this interesting subject, by a person of my profession and experience, might prove of some advantage to the public, among whom, it appears, much ignorance and misapprehension prevails, and whose opinion has been in a high degree misled by imperfect, and, in many instances, erroneous statements, published of late, at home, by persons led astray by a misguided religious zeal, and who took upon themselves to treat of matters with which they were scarcely at all, or but very imperfectly acquainted.

In fact, on perusing the reports of those gentlemen, persons unacquainted with the subject might be induced to suppose, that the Hindoos are a people quite prepared for a revolution in their religious system, and ready to break to pieces and trample upon their gods of stone and brass. One would think, in hearing them, that these fields "*are white already to harvest,*" and that it is only necessary to come with sickles and baskets to cut down and gather an abundant crop.

For my part, as an experienced veteran in this kind of sacred militia, engaged for a long period in the same kind of holy warfare, thoroughly acquainted with the character, the dispositions, and resources of the common foe, and with all the difficulties which are to be met with in the contest, I beg to be allowed to entertain the most serious doubts of the truth of those pompous and all-promising reports, until more unbiassed and more impartial evidence shall have removed my scepticism.

It only remains to me to solicit your kind indulgence, chiefly on account of the bad style in which these letters are written; and moreover to express to you my regret that it is not in my power to do more ample justice to the subject, owing to a want of ability, and also to the difficulty I had to contend with in discussing the matter in a language which is not my own, and with which I am but very imperfectly acquainted.

I have stated with candour, with simplicity, and freedom, all that I thought capable of interesting the public, and all that appeared to me worthy of being known, as I supposed that a person of my experience might speak without restraint on a subject which is his peculiar province, and on which many have already given much erroneous information to the public.

I have the honour to be, &c. &c.

16*th November*, 1816.

# VINDICATION

OF THE

# HINDOOS,

BOTH MALES AND FEMALES,

IN ANSWER TO THE ATTACKS MADE UPON BOTH BY

THE REVEREND ———.

## *Extract of a Letter from the Rev. —— to Major W. C. at Calcutta.*

My dear Sir,

I WILL candidly confess to you that the highly exaggerated accounts of the Rev. —— and the severity with which he treats these poor Hindoos, are far from being a subject of edification to me. I have, at different times, perused many of the public accounts of the new reformers of several sects, settled of late in several parts of India, communicated to their correspondents in England, and I cannot disguise to you that their exaggerations and misrepresentations (not to use harsher terms) respecting the Hindoos have been to me a subject of much scandal, and have, in several instances, roused my indignation to a high degree.

In fact, from their reports, I see that those gentlemen particularly delight in representing these people under the blackest and most odious colours. With them the Hindoos are nothing but barbarians; a people loaded with every kind of vice, without a single spark of virtue. Not only their religion, but also their system of civilization, their character, their public and domestic institutions; all their usages and practices are indiscriminately branded with infamy, and held forth to public contempt; and they themselves are abused, reviled, and degraded almost to the level of brutes.

Such is, as far as I can judge from their public reports, the view taken of these people by most of the new reformers at present settled among them.

But I am happy to know that a quite different view of the subject has been taken by a Warren Hastings, a Burke, a Cornwallis, a Robertson, a Sir William Jones, a Colebrooke, a Hawkins, a Wilkins, and many other enlightened persons who had made close and deep researches on all that relates to the Hindoos. I am happy to know that such men of talents, in acknowledging the vices of the Hindoos, had candor enough to acknowledge also their virtues, and to make a just estimate of what was good, and what was bad in their institutions. Now it is a subject of regret to see that the opinions and authority of so many enlightened and independent persons are disregarded, to listen to the suspicious accounts, and wild theories of men of mediocrity, who have of late undertaken the altogether impracticable task of reforming these nations in their religion, morals, and manners.

I am also happy that, in my humble sphere, and obscure station, an experience of thirty years, passed in an unrestrained intercourse with these people, has taught me a quite different theory, and to view the subject in a much more favourable light. I am happy to the end of my researches to find that, in witnessing among them many disgusting vices, I have been able to discover also many eminent virtues.

It is true that some of my critics have accused me of being tinctured with Hinduism, and strongly biassed in favour of the Hindoos, because in describing their vices and bad qualities I had also presumed to take notice of their virtues and good qualities; but the fact is, that if I have any thing to reproach myself with in my writings on the subject of the Hindoos, it is to have been rather too severe in finding faults with them in matters which would perhaps have been a subject of praise to more unbiassed authors.

In perusing the pamphlet of the Rev. ——, I have been sorry to see that able writer so violently prejudiced against the Hindoos. Such a virulent style as he employs has appeared to me very little becoming a person of his profession. When I see him boldly asserting that "in every relation of man to man, the natives of India are thoroughly depraved;" that "in this pagan nation we have the absence of all virtue, "and the disposition to every vice;" that "in ignorance, in vice, and immorality, the Hindoos are far below the most savage nations:" when I see him making the quite erroneous insinuations, that "a chaste female is almost unknown among the Hindoos;" that "the Hindoo females have not a spark of maternal tenderness towards their offspring;" and many other no less shocking and untenable paradoxes, I am at a loss to account for such misrepresentations,—for such a blindness. It is not the blindness of prejudice or religious zeal; it is the blindness of passion and animosity.

Unfortunately those new reformers come from Europe to India very strongly prejudiced against the Hindoos, and with the presumptuous hope that they shall be able to operate, in the religious and civil habits of the latter, reforms and changes which have at all times baffled the utmost endeavours of the best disposed persons. On their arrival in the country they continue to look at these people with

European eyes, and European prejudices, and to act accordingly; but finding themselves disappointed in all their attempts to make an impression upon them on the score of religion, or otherwise, they, in their fiery zeal, or rather in their despair, avenge themselves by lavishing every kind of abuse and insult not only on their religion, but also on all their institutions both public and private, sacred and profane. I cannot disguise to you that I see with a kind of indignation that these peaceable and submissive people have of late years been made a kind of target, to aim at them the shafts of calumny and malevolence, and to debase them by the most unfair means.

On the other hand, the methods devised by the new reformers to make an impression upon these pagan nations, are, in my humble opinion, the most absurd, and most ridiculous which could be contrived. Fancying that in order to convert the Hindoos to Christianity, it was only necessary to lay the Bible before them, they at their first outset made extremely incorrect, and almost unintelligible translations of our sacred books into the several idioms of the country. Our disfigured Holy Scriptures were profusely diffused among the inhabitants under such a contemptible garb, and upon this only foundation the latter were angrily required to shift for themselves, to build their faith, and reform their religion, civilization, and manners.

I will confess that I understand nothing of such a mode of improving the condition of the senations. Alas! it is not Bibles the poor Hindoos want or ask for. It is food and raiment. When the belly is empty, and the back bare, the best disposed even among the Christians feel themselves but very little inclined to peruse the Bible. Every day some of my distressed followers call upon me, the males to show me their tattered *cumbelees*, and the females their ragged clothes, exclaiming "*Samy! bettleyaghee eerootenee bouddy*," *I am naked, please your reverence*; and soliciting assistance; but no one comes to say to me that he wants a Bible. If in those circumstances I dismissed them after. having made them a present of a Bible, I apprehend that the poor creatures would find the sacred book a very sad substitute for their real wants.

I will not fear to declare, that it is to me a subject of scandal to observe, that while so much anxiety is evinced to supply the Hindoos with Bibles which they never asked for, and which cannot be to them of the least utility, no voice is raised to supply their actual necessities, and procure them food and clothing, which they ask so clamorously.

Our good ancestors, who, with perhaps a little less learning than their offspring, had much more good sense, never thought of improving the condition of the pagan nations, by intruding the Bible among them. They invariably taught us that the exercise of that truly sublime virtue *charity* consisted in assisting the needy, feeding the hungry, and clothing the naked. Now in this age of light, we are taught a quite new theory, and told that there is another charitable duty paramount to all, which consists in circulating the Bible among the pagans; and while thousands are yearly dying from starvation in England and India, hundreds of thousands of pounds are subscribed for the purpose of distributing the Bible among the heathen nations. I am at a loss to account for such an infatuation. It is, in my humble opinion, a new discovery which the 19th century will have very little room to glory in hereafter.

I beg that you will not be scandalized at this frank and candid expression of my sentiments. I thank God that I am as firm, as sincere, and as undisguised a believer in the truth of the Christian religion, and in the divine origin of the holy books from which it derives its sacred tenets, as the warmest supporter of the Bible-society; but the attempts to enlighten the pagan Hindoos by the circulation of the Bible among them have at all times appeared to me so palpably absurd, that I could never make up my mind to such a mode of bringing them to sounder notions on religion.

It appears, however, that the new reformers begin to be sensible of the impossibility of making an impression on these pagan nations with respect to religion, and in their despair of succeeding in the attempt, they have now altered their plan, and turned their views to another object. Their only ambition at present seems to be to remove the clouds of ignorance which hang over these people, and instil into their minds principles of civilization, morality, and pure manners.

But I will take the liberty to ask those well wishers to the improvement of the natives of India, is it the Hindoos or ourselves who stand in need of reform on these several matters? The former are at present become as fully aware of our vices, our immorality, and looseness of manners, as we are of theirs. What is then, and what will at all times be the answer of a Hindoo of common sense to an Englishman or a Frenchman who will presume to come forward for the purpose of reforming or changing his education and manners, and to speak to him of morality and of the superiority of his own institutions and civilization?

"You speak, gentlemen, (will the proud Hindoo reply,) of morality, and of purity of manners, and you boast of a great superiority over me in these respects. But pray, how comes it, that, from the very accounts you are not ashamed to publish even in this my supposed thoroughly corrupted country, it appears, that in each of your respective metropolises, London and Paris, you reckon no less than forty thousand prostitutes who keep public shops of infamy, and live by the most unruly dissoluteness? Look, gentlemen, to Calcutta, Madras, and Bombay, and see whether you will be able to find such an extensive sink of corruption, and so large a proportion of vice, among the crowded population of these large cities.

"You speak in high terms of your civilization, of your refined education and manners, but how comes it, that, amidst the advantages you claim over me in these respects, crimes and vices of every kind are more prevalent in your countries than in mine? From whence comes it, that, with the superior education and civilization you boast of, your cities and towns are filled with thieves, sharpers, pickpockets, swindlers, gamblers, forgers, false-coiners, and other knaves of every description, most of them happily unknown in my supposed thoroughly corrupted country, who set at defiance the most strict vigilance of a very severe police, and whose numbers are daily increasing? How comes it, that your high roads are so much infested by robbers, murderers, and assassins, and that every kind of crime increases to such an alarming extent, that your prisons and houses of correction are scarcely sufficient to contain the number of malefactors every day committed to them?

"You boast of pure and refined manners, but how comes it, that habitual drunkenness is so prevailing among the lower ranks of your community, and whoredom amongst the higher, without these vices seeming to excite any sense of shame or remorse in those who are addicted to them.

"Believe me, gentlemen, (will the headstrong Hindoo add,) as long as you continue to exercise your sway over us with justice, moderation, and humanity, you will find us a peaceable and submissive people; but do not speak of intruding your system of civilization, your education and manners on us, because you will never succeed in convincing us, that they are superior to ours; still less will you prevail upon us to adopt them. We do not stand in want of so wretched a present."

Such is in substance the answer I have almost invariably received from the Hindoos of good sense of all castes, whenever I have presumed to speak to them of our superiority in civilization and education, in morals and manners; and their observations have appeared to me so just and unanswerable, that I have for a long time desisted from obtruding myself on their attention on the subject.

It has at present become a kind of fashion to speak of improvements and ameliorations in the civilization and institutions of the Hindoos, and every one has his own plans for effecting them; but if we could for an instant lay aside our European eyes and European prejudices, and look at the Hindoos with some degree of impartiality, we should perhaps find that they are nearly our equals in all that is good, and our inferiors only in all that is bad.

In my humble opinion, these people have reached the degree of civilization that is consistent with their climate, their wants, their natural dispositions, and physical constitution; and in fact, in education, in manners, in accomplishments, and in the discharge of social duties, I believe them superior to some European nations, and scarcely inferior to any. In all these respects, I believe them superior to the Turks and Russians, while they are only surpassed by the persons above the middle ranks in other countries, and they are at least equal, if not superior, to the common ranks in England and France. If you will take the trouble to attend to the subject, and examine with impartiality the character and conduct of the persons of the same condition in our countries and in India, and compare husbandman to husbandman, artificer to artificer, mechanic to mechanic, &c. &c., I apprehend that you will find that, in education and manners, the Hindoo shines far above the European.

In order to be convinced of the superiority of the manners of the common ranks among the Hindoos over those of the same description of persons among the Europeans, we only need attend to the conduct and habits of both in their mutual intercourse in society.

Let four Europeans assemble together to transact business, or for any other purpose; their first and common thought, in such circumstances, will almost invariably be an appeal to the bottle, in which they will, in most instances, indulge to excess. Their most trifling business, as well as their social intercourse, must always be carried on in the midst of cups, to which they will recur, until, being deprived of the use of their reason, their assemblies degenerate into the most disgusting scenes of confusion, and often terminate in quarrels and fighting.

Let a European of common rank, who has rendered you service, call upon you to receive his reward. After you have paid him his just salary, he will seldom fail to make an appeal to your generosity, and ask you a further remuneration. Ask him for what purpose. To drink, will he answer, or, in other terms, to get drunk.

Look, on the other side, at the conduct of the Hindoos in the very same circumstances; their only anxiety, their only delight will be to have a few leaves of betel, and they will be fully satisfied by chewing this exhilarating aromatic plant. This harmless gratification is the only sensual enjoyment they covet in their social intercourse. The proposal alone of using intoxicating liquors would be considered by all as the grossest of insults, and instantly be resented as such. I now ask on which side is the purity of manners?

You can convince yourself, in a still more striking manner, of the superiority of the education and manners of the common classes of society in India over the same classes in Europe, by comparing the conduct and habits of our soldiers and sailors with those of the sepoys and ship's lascars; the former, like beasts, cannot be kept within the bounds of duty but by blows, and the severest discipline. They cannot, in general, be allowed the least indulgence, or the least degree of freedom, without abusing it, by giving themselves up to excesses. On the other hand, their private low habits, and their total disregard of all decorum, are a subject of disgust, not to say of horror, to the vile pariahs themselves, who are the only class of Hindoos who dare approach them.

Behold, on the other side, your sepoy and ship's lascar, and you will at all times find his behaviour, both public and private, orderly, peaceable, and becoming; and seldom will you find him offending against public decorum.

Even amongst the lowest rabble, with the Hindoos, you will never witness any thing approaching to those shocking scenes of scandal, to that total disregard of decency and decorum, which are daily exhibited in alehouses and gin-shops in England, and in *cabarets* and *gargotes* in France.

On the other hand, the Hindoos are not in want of improvement in the discharge of social duties among themselves. They understand this point as well as, and perhaps better than the Europeans. They might even be said to be rather excessive in this respect in several instances. They will never suffer the needy who has implored their charity to go unassisted. Their hospitality among themselves, it is well known, has no bounds. Even the humble, the distressed pariah, as long as he has a measure of grain in his possession, will cheerfully share his pap of millet with the weary traveller of his caste who may happen to take shelter in his hut; and in all their wants and distresses the Hindoos, of all castes, will readily assist each other more effectually than the Europeans would do in the same circumstances. What the European possesses he keeps for himself. What the Hindoo possesses he is always disposed to share with those who have nothing. In fact, it might be said that a wealthy Hindoo considers himself as the depositary, or the distributor, rather than the proprietor of his fortune, so greatly prone is he to acts of charity and benevolence; and it is chiefly from this cause that those frequent revolutions in the fortunes of the Hindoos, and those frequent passages from extreme opulence to extreme poverty, arise.

It cannot, however, be denied that the Hindoos are more generally disposed to knavery, dishonesty, and their concomitant vices, than the Europeans. The propensity of most of them to pilfering, for instance, is almost irresistible; and, in general, if a native can avoid discovery in being dishonest, he will be so as often as his own interests require it. I cannot, however, attribute these evils to a perversity of character peculiar to themselves; and, in my humble opinion, these vices have their origin only in the extreme poverty common to the great majority of the Hindoos. To persons in the least acquainted with human nature, it is needless to say that there is no stronger incitement to dishonesty than poverty. Europeans, in general, are more honest than the Hindoos, because they live comparatively in easier and more independent circumstances; but, on a close attention to the subject, it will perhaps be found that, among an equal number of distressed people, the proportion of determined rogues is greater in Europe than in India.

Your modern reformers seem to be of opinion, that in order to render these people happy and virtuous, it is only necessary to civilize and enlighten them. But the history of ancient and modern times bears testimony that it is not always the best civilized and most enlightened nations that are the most virtuous and the most just.

" Ignorance (says the Rev. ——) is the parent of poverty, &c." It might be said with equal justness, " Poverty is the parent of ignorance." Such a reasoning is nothing, merely a *petitio principii*, or *circulus vitiosus*, to which I can perceive no opening or issue. The reverend gentleman's reasoning would have been more logical and satisfactory, had he said, " The poverty of the Hindoos, and the vices derived from it, originate in their natural indolence and apathy, and the latter proceed from the climate or elements under which they live, and over which we can exercise no kind of control or influence."

The Rev. —— asserts, that " dishonesty is so familiar to the natives, that a Hindoo will never trust another." This assertion, especially the latter part of it, is one of the most unfounded that was ever brought forward against these people. If any well grounded accusation may be brought against them on this head, it is that they are rather too confident, and too little distrustful in their transactions and dealings with each other.

It is a known fact that those who are in easy circumstances among them often lend money, sometimes to a large amount, to persons of their acquaintance, without witnesses, and without written bond or other vouchers; and it is uncommon to see a debt contracted in this private manner denied even by a debtor in distress. He will, it is true, use every kind of cunning and craft to avoid payment, or to obtain a delay from his creditor. He will, perhaps, furtively run away to escape from his molestations; but rarely will he altogether deny the debt.

It is also a known fact, that merchants are obliged to sell their goods privately at credit, to at least a half of their customers, but it is rare to see the latter, although reduced to the last degree of misery, deny their obligations to the merchant.

It is likewise a known fact that servants, on a salary of eight or ten shillings per mensem, are often intrusted by their masters with large sums of money, and sent to their correspondents at a distance of, perhaps, two or three hundred miles or further, to purchase goods, or for other purposes; and instances of persons in such circumstances running away with the money intrusted to their care, or otherwise embezzling it, are very rare.

It is also a known fact, of which repeated instances have come within my personal observation, that people in time of alarm, or of great disturbances, in the places of their residence, being under the necessity of emigrating to more settled countries, secretly deposit, before their departure, in some place of safety, under the charge of some person of their acquaintance, money, jewels, and other valuables, sometimes to a large amount, and breaches of trust on the part of the latter, by embezzling the property secretly deposited with them, happen very seldom. I have known many instances of persons in such circumstances returning after an absence of several years, and finding their property untouched, although intrusted to the charge of persons who were themselves living in a state of distress.

Such instances are not, certainly, proofs of distrust in the one, or of dishonesty in the other.

From what I have heard or read from time to time, it would appear that a ferment is now at work in Calcutta, and a revolution in the habits and manners of the Hindoos near at hand. If it be really the case, I apprehend that that ferment is rather of a mischievous kind, and that it will operate a change for the worse. For my part, I shall certainly be the last man to interfere with the civil usages and habits, with the social institutions and manners of the Hindoos, and will never join those who employ themselves to make the extremely perilous experiment of changing their national customs and manners for those of Europe; and as a friend of yours, my dear Sir, I shall surely never advise you, after the knowledge I have obtained of the character of the Hindoos, to trust, in any capacity whatever, a native who has renounced, or who slights the usages of his caste, or the prejudices of the country. I shall, above all, never advise you to make such a man your butler, or your treasurer. In the former case, you would soon find that your liquors were fast wasting, and in the latter, you would, ere long, find a large deficit in your chest. For, you may at the first outset, and without farther enquiries, judge, that a person of this description is a quite lost character, and that his first steps to improvement, after having renounced the usages and prejudices of his caste, will be to turn a drunkard and a rogue. The more nice and scrupulous a native is in the observance of his usages and practices, both religious and profane, the more worthy will he prove of your trust and confidence. Such is the result of my observations on the subject during a period of more than thirty years.

In the mean while, I can hardly believe, that the ferment which is said to agitate the mind of the public in Calcutta, and some other places, works to such an extent as some people conceive; still less can I expect from this source any amelioration in the condition of the Hindoos. In our last interview, you mentioned to me, I believe, that the agitation produced of late in the public, on this subject, was in a great measure owing to the exertions of the learned Brahmin, Rammohun-Roy, to enlighten and enlarge the minds of his countrymen. I have perused a few of the essays of that Brahmin; they are only an exposition of the doctrine of the school called *Védantam*, the most followed of the six sects, into which are divided the Hindoos who make profession of learning. Rammohun-Roy teaches us nothing new, when he says, that the present worship of the Hindoos differs widely from the primitive religion of their ancestors. This is a fact pretty generally known at present. At the same time, the prevailing worship of India is so deeply rooted, that it would require other powers, and other means, than those possessed by that Brahmin, to bring back the bulk of the nation to the much less unreasonable worship of their first ancestors.

In the mean time, from what I have seen of the writings of that reformer Brahmin, I apprehend that his talents have been much over-rated, and the unqualified encomiums bestowed upon him from several quarters very little deserved; but, when I observed him, at an entertainment he recently gave to the Spaniards living in Calcutta, presuming to give a decided opinion on the late revolution in Spain, and emphatically boasting, in an elaborate speech, published with an equal emphasis in most of the public papers at that presidency, the advantages of religious and political *freedom*, (a word, the meaning of which, I apprehend, he does not understand,) he sank still lower in my estimation. In fact, to see a Brahmin decorated with the *treble cord*, that indubitable badge of the most oppressive and most degrading despotism, turn the apostle of freedom, is so shocking an anomaly, that persons acquainted with the subject will find it difficult to reconcile themselves to such a contradiction.

On the other hand, the anxiety evinced by the natives (as you observe in your letter) to attend the schools set up in several places, does not prove, in my humble opinion, that they are desirous to attain real learning, and improve their minds by literary endowments.

They go to those schools for the sole purpose of attaining a competent acquaintance with the English language, in order to be able, by this means, to gain a livelihood, as this accomplishment is at present the only way to attain an honourable and advantageous situation in the several offices of government. As soon as they have attained their object, all is over with your books of science and morality, they never more cast a look at them during their lives.

You may convince yourself of this fact by your own observations. There are, I suppose, in Calcutta, many hundred natives of all castes, who can read, write, and speak English well; among them, I am persuaded, that you will not be able to find ten independent individuals who are ever seen with an English book of science in their hands.

Public schools were also established about a century ago at Pondicherry, by the French Jesuit missionaries, and at Trankebar by the Protestant ones, for the purpose of teaching the natives both the European and the native languages, and they are still in existence; but I have never heard of this mode of instruction having operated any material change or reform in the national prejudices, or in the habits and manners of the pupils educated in those schools.

Respecting the schools set up in many parts of the country, for the purpose of teaching the native languages, I am of opinion that the natives are by no means deficient in this respect, and that they do not stand in need of our interference on the subject. There are very few villages in which one or many public schools are not to be found. If you object to me that the system of instruction pursued in those schools is defective, without entering into a discussion on that point, I will content myself with answering, that the students learn in them all that is necessary to their ranks and wants, and all that is taught to persons of their condition, in the village-schools set up in our respective countries, namely, reading, writing, and accounts; no more is certainly necessary for ninety-nine hundredths of the vast population of India; and their extreme poverty will not allow the great majority among them to attain even these humble accomplishments.

If you object to me that what I have stated in this letter seems to be in several points at variance with what I have stated in my former writings, in which I have not in several cases expressed so favorable an opinion on the Hindoos as I do at present, I will answer, that in my former productions most of my censures, if not all, are directed, first, against the Brahmins, or other persons who like them live by imposture, and the whole of whom do not form a twentieth of the population of India. In all times, and in all countries, imposture and knavery have almost always been inseparable companions.

Secondly, my censures are also directed against the enormities of the monstrous worship prevailing in the country, to which it has at all times been impossible for me to reconcile myself.

However, if it were in our power, through fair means, to take off from the religion of the country several monstrosities which are truly a disgrace to human nature, I would forgive them all that is only extravagant in their worship. Those monstrosities are but too well known to me. Nobody deplores them more bitterly than I do, and few have laboured more hard than I have to remove them; but seeing all my efforts for the purpose of no avail, I have contented myself (according to the instructions of our divine teacher on the subject) with "wiping off the dust of my shoes on those obstinate unbelievers," and with recommending them to the paternal care of the Father of mercies, leaving their final judgment in the hands of him to whom alone the professors of all religions are accountable for their faith. In the mean while, the blindness and obduracy of my hearers so far from exciting my hatred, have, on the contrary, given rise to feelings of compassion and good will towards them.

I have just hinted, that if it were in our power, through fair means, to take off from the religion of the Hindoos its enormities, we ought perhaps to stop there, and overlook all that is only extravagant in their worship, because the minds of these people are composed of such materials, that they cannot be roused except by extravagancies; and, after all, we must be disposed to overlook in others the defects from which we are not entirely free ourselves; for, what is the kind of worship upon which extravagancies, under some shape or other, may not be charged by the opposite party? You, for instance, as a Protestant, cannot fail to find out, in the Catholic religion, tenets and practices which will prove to you a subject of censure, while they are to me, a most sincere Catholic, a subject of edification.

But I believe that you, a sober Protestant, and I, a tolerant Catholic, shall agree in expressing our common disgust, or at least our dislike, at several striking extravagancies prevailing among some Christian sects, and which appear an open insult to good sense. I believe, for instance, that we should scarcely be able to keep a serious countenance, if we witnessed the groans, the grimaces, and wild convulsions, the jumpings, kickings, howlings, &c. which are observed in the religious assemblies of the Jumpers, Shakers, Methodists, Quakers, Ranters, &c. For an account of the latter, the *Ranters*, who are a new sect sprung up of late in England, see the *Monthly Magazine* for May, 1820, p. 297, 298.; and if you wish to have a curious account of the religious exercises of the Quakers, see the *Quarterly Review*, No. XLI., p. 145, 146.; and after you have perused so disgusting an account, I boldly defy you to find out any thing among the bands of Baheraghees, Dassaroo, Andy, and other Hindoo fanatics who flock to the temples of Teeroopatty and Jagghernat, which may be compared with the scenes of extravagance and madness, exhibited by that sect of Christians in their religious assemblies; and yet these enthusiastic Christians are a very honest people, and rather scrupulous in the discharge of all moral and social duties.

Let it not, however, be supposed that I mean to excuse or palliate the grossness of the Hindoo idolatry, or to deny that the credulity of these nations, in religious matters, is carried to a degree of debasement and stupidity, which has scarcely any parallel; but even on this point I dare to maintain that we outdo them in several instances; and I am of opinion, that it ill behoves us to deride the Hindoos on the score of absurd credulity, when we see, in this very century, a country which boasts of holding the first rank in civilization, education, learning, and manners, give birth to a pseudo-prophetess of the name of Johanna Southcote, who, after announcing herself as the woman destined to crush the head of the serpent mentioned in the Scriptures, and as being pregnant with the Messiah, gained over to her party thousands of proselytes, among whom were to be found several persons of rank and education. I question whether an instance of more debasing and stupid credulity could be quoted among the most superstitious Hindoos.

I have also many times heard prejudiced Europeans endeavouring to vilify the Hindoos, and supporting their opinion on the subject, by the looseness of manners, and lascivious deportment of the country dancing girls.

Nothing appeared to them more indecent, or better calculated to pollute the mind and corrupt the heart, than the postures and the dances of those courtezans. I have sometimes been under the necessity of witnessing the song and dances of those prostitutes in public assemblies, but I do not hesitate to declare, that none of their steps or postures have appeared to me so intentionally lascivious, and so shamefully indecorous, as those of our actresses, when performing their parts on our stages; and you will, perhaps, smile at my simplicity, when I venture to say that none of their dances have appeared to me so highly indecent as that new European dance, known under the name of Waltz, at present become a favourite in our countries.

It is thus that we are always disposed " to behold a mote that is in our brother's eye, but consider not the beam that is in our own eye."

" Il y a, (says Montesquieu, Esp. des Lois, lib. xxiv. ch. 24.) beaucoup des lois locales dans les diverses religions, et quand Montezuma s'obstinoit à dire que la religion des Espagnols étoit bonne pour leur pays, et celle du Mexique pour le sien, il ne disoit pas une absurdité; parcequ'en effet les législateurs n'ont pu s'empêcher d'avoir égard à ce que la nature avoit établi avant eux."

I am far, very far indeed, from admitting all the consequences which might be drawn from the principles laid by that illustrious author in the quoted passage, by which he seems to hint, that religion is a mere matter of geography. Let nobody suppose that I have quoted the above words, as if I considered the monstrous religion of the Hindoos as a matter of necessity or indifference. I again repeat, that I pity, I love, I cherish the idolatrous Hindoos; but I abhor their idolatry. The fact is, however, that the very words of of Montezuma to the Spaniards have been repeated to me a hundred times by the Hindoos, Brahmins, and others, in my religious controversies with them. It was ordinarily by the words of that Mexican emperor they put an end to the dispute, exclaiming with much emphasis, "After all, your religion is good for your country, and ours is good for India."

On the whole, from all that has come within my knowledge, I observe, with sorrow, that the interference of the new reformers to improve the condition of the Hindoos has thus far produced more evil than good. In support of this assertion, I will content myself with citing the two following striking instances.

The first relates to the burning of widows on the pile of their deceased husbands. It is an indubitable fact, fully confirmed by the official reports of the local magistrates, that since the clamours raised in Europe and India, and since the country-government has judged fit to interfere, to a certain degree, in order to render it less frequent, it has come more into fashion, and more prevalent. I have seen lists of the victims devoting themselves to that cruel superstition; and I have observed, that in the districts of Calcutta and Benarez, where the horrid practice is most common, the number of victims has been of late much greater than it was about twelve years ago, when the natives were left to themselves, and nobody presumed to interfere with their customs.

The second instance is more within my province and personal observation. It is a certain fact, that since the new reformers have overflowed the country with their Bibles and religious tracts, the Christian religion, and the natives who profess it, have become more odious to the heathen than ever. Formerly the native Christians, when known, were, it is true, despised and shunned by the pagans;

but, on account of their small numbers, they were scarcely noticed. Now the religious tracts, dispersed with profusion in every direction, have brought them into public notice, and rendered them an object of universal opprobrium; and, I apprehend, that this very cause would already have given rise to an open persecution, were it not for the awe inspired by a government, which is well known to extend an equal protection to all religious worship.

All know that nothing is better calculated to produce irritation, opposition, and resistance, than contradiction; above all, when the contradicted party is the strongest and most obstinate. Now, such is precisely the effect produced by the interference of the new reformers with the prejudices of the Hindoos; and I have reason to apprehend, that the opposition of the latter will increase in proportion to the extent of the contradictions to which they may be exposed, until it shall finish by some explosion, which may make all India a theatre of confusion and anarchy, to which it will be in the power of no government to apply a remedy.

Such is, my dear Sir, the view I have taken of the subject. I could go to a much fuller extent; but, as you have already seen my writings on the same matter, and as you told me in our last interview, that you expected to have an opportunity to peruse my new manuscript on the Hindoos, in which you will find more satisfactory details, I will conclude this already too prolix letter, to which you are at full liberty to give such publicity as you wish. I only regret that I am not endowed with sufficient talents to do more ample justice to the subject, and vindicate with more ability the wrongs of the too much abused and injured Hindoos.

I remain, &c. &c.

*From my Mata near Seringapatam,*
*15th December*, 1820.

## *Vindication of the Hindoo Females.*

To Captain M. C.

My dear Sir,

We had, until these latter times, been almost uniformly taught by both ancient and modern historians, who have written on India and its inhabitants, to look on the Hindoos as a mild, sober, industrious, forbearing, patient, and submissive people, who although possessing a system of political government quite original, and having no parallel in any other nation on earth, had, nevertheless, reached a reasonable height on the scale of civilization, cultivated the arts with some success, made tolerable progress in some branches of the highest sciences, such as astronomy, philosophy, ethics, &c. &c., established among themselves, through the division of castes, a system of subordination and order, which, by assigning in the most precise manner to each individual his rank and duties in the great community, allowed nobody to remain idle, and provided in the most efficacious manner for the wants of the whole; as a people living under a form of government founded on so solid a basis that no human effort, no kind of opposition or oppression had been able to subvert, or even to shake it.

The enquiries of many enlightened and judicious authors of several nations, who in more modern times had visited the country, and made an attentive study of the character, manners, and customs of these people, as well as of the system of civilization established among them, had generally served to strengthen the favourable opinion already entertained of them; and I am happy to have it in my power to declare, that close and impartial researches on the subject, during a period of thirty years of free and unrestrained intercourse among the natives of all ranks and classes, have had the effect of producing the same favourable impressions on my own mind.

It was reserved for a few enthusiasts, who have of late years made their appearance in the country, under the imposing title of reformers, to reverse this pleasing picture, by giving us the most shocking accounts on the subject, and by holding out to our view, the mild and inoffensive Hindoos, as a people wholly polluted by every kind of wickedness; as a race of barbarians sunk into the deepest abyss of ignorance and immorality; as a people far below the most savage nations, and approaching nearer, by their beastly habits and unnatural vices, to the brute than the human creation.

If you have perused the pamphlets published of late at home, by the Rev. ——, and above all, his address to the ladies of Liverpool, you will have observed, that all these and many other no less degrading, odious, and false notions are fully upheld, and boldly professed by that gentleman.

Having in a former letter adverted to another attack, made by that author on the Hindoos in general, I will content myself in this, with reviewing his illiberal aspersions of the Hindoo females.

The Rev. Gentleman begins his attacks on the Hindoo fair sex, by stating, that "women in India are in a state of ignorance and degradation, which has no parallel in the history of tribes the most savage and barbarous;" and some lines farther he says, that "a Hindoo female is, in fact, a mere animal kept for burthen or slaughter in the house of her husband. Her life spent in an inanity and idleness, which prepare her for a life doomed to be spent in superstition and vice," &c. &c.

Let us consider now with a mind unbiassed by passion or prejudice, whether the Hindoo females deserve the odious aspersions cast upon them by that author, and whether they are held in that low state of degradation, ignorance, and inanity, which would render their condition scarcely superior to that of brutes.

No one can be more displeased than I am, with that austerity of manners which has drawn so marked a line of separation between the two sexes, and denied women in India a due share in the social intercourse and a proper attention to the improvement of their intellectual faculties; but it is well known that the same line of demarcation between the sexes, and the same austerity of manners, have from the earliest to the present times existed among all oriental nations. The conduct of the latter in this respect may originate in physical and moral causes till now unexplained, or but imperfectly known to us, and perhaps also to that spirit of jealousy and stubbornness common to all weak minds, and inherent in a particular manner in all oriental people.

The Rev. —— affirms that this exclusion of women from a free social intercourse with men is peculiar to the pagan nations, and does not exist amongst any people who have been enlightened by the light of Revelation. This assertion is inaccurate: it is a known fact that the same exclusion prevails, with nearly equal rigour, among all the Oriental Christian nations. It prevails among the Armenians, Georgians, Abyssinians, the Copts of Egypt, and the Greeks; and it prevailed, with more or less severity, not more than fifty or sixty years ago, among the Spaniards and Portuguese. It was only in those chivalrous times which originated in the Crusades, and were afterwards so much enhanced by the French *Troubadours*, that the females began to be put on a footing of equality with the males in the best civilized countries of Europe; and that system of courtship to which the refined modern manners have added so many charms introduced: but these improvements in the condition of the European females have nothing, or very little, to do with Christianity.

On the other hand, it may be said, with truth, that so far are the Hindoo females from being held in that low state of contempt and degradation in which the Rev. —— repeatedly describes them in his letter, that, on the contrary, they lie under much less restraint, enjoy more real freedom, and are in possession of more enviable privileges than the persons of their sex in any other Asiatic country. In fact, to them belong the entire management of their household, the care of their children, the superintendence of the menial servants, the distribution of alms and charities. To their charge are generally intrusted the money, jewels, and other valuables. To them belongs the care of procuring provisions, and providing for all expences. It is they also who are charged, almost to the exclusion of their husbands, with the most important affair of procuring wives for their sons, and husbands for their daughters; and, in doing this, they evince a niceness, an attention, and foresight, which are not certainly surpassed in any country; while, in the management of their domestic business, they in general show a shrewdness, a savingness, and an intelligence which would do honour to the best housewives in Europe.

In the mean while, the austerity and roughness with which they are outwardly treated in public, by their husbands, is rather a matter of form, and entirely ceases when the husband and his wife are in private. It is then that the Hindoo females assume all that empire which is every where exercised, in civilized countries, by the persons of their sex over the male part of creation; find means to bring them under their subjection, and rule over them, in several instances, with a despotic sway. In short, although outwardly exposed in public to the forbidding and repulsive frowns of an austere husband, they can be considered in no other light than as perfectly the mistresses within the house.

The influence of the Hindoo females on the welfare of families is so well known, that the successes or misfortunes of the Hindoos are almost entirely attributed to their good or bad management. When a person prospers in the world, it is customary to say that he has the happiness to possess an intelligent wife, to whom he is indebted for his welfare; and when any one runs to ruin, it is the custom to say that he has for his partner a bad wife, to whom his misfortunes must chiefly be attributed. In short, a good-natured and intelligent wife is considered, by all castes of natives, as the most valuable of all the blessings which could be bestowed on a family, and a bad one as the most dreaded of all curses; so great is their influence on the fate of the Hindoo households.

The authority of married women within

their houses is chiefly exerted in preserving good order and peace among the persons who compose their families; and a great many among them discharge this important duty with a prudence and a discretion which have scarcely a parallel in Europe. I have known families composed of between thirty and forty persons, or more, consisting of grown sons and daughters, all married and all having children, living together under the superintendence of an old matron — their mother or mother-in-law. The latter, by good management, and by accommodating herself to the temper of her daughters-in-law; by using, according to circumstances, firmness or forbearance, succeeded in preserving peace and harmony during many years amongst so many females, who had all jarring interests, and still more jarring tempers. I ask you whether it would be possible to attain the same end, in the same circumstances, in our countries, where it is scarcely possible to make two women living under the same roof to agree together.

It is true that the same spirit of concord between an old Hindoo matron and her daughters on one side, and her daughters-in law on the other, does not prevail in an equal degree in all households; but instances of such union and harmony are by no means uncommon, and they last to the death of their parents; when, ordinarily, the brothers divide the heritage, separate with their several families, and each one shifts for himself.

The Rev. —— remarks, that a Hindoo female "is despised as soon as born by her parents and friends, disappointed that the child is not a boy," &c. If he had contented himself with merely stating that the birth of a boy causes, in general, more joy to parents than that of a girl, I should have overlooked this passage of his letter; as it is a weakness common to all nations, and from which the Hindoos are not exempt, to hail with more exultation the birth of a male than that of a female, and Hindoo parents are in a greater degree under the influence of this feeling, because they derive more support from a son than from a daughter; but it is untrue that a female is despised and spurned by her parents as soon as born. Parents, chiefly mothers, foster their children, both males and females, with an equal tenderness. So far from females being despised while living under the paternal roof, their parents and brothers are often seen submitting themselves to severe privations for the purpose of procuring trinkets and jewels for their daughters or sisters, in order that they may be able to appear in public with decency and advantage, while the males are seen in rags or half naked, and live forgotten at home.

The principal care of parents is to procure suitable establishments for their daughters, over whom mothers continue to exercise a kind of paramount authority, even after their marriage, being particularly attentive to check that despotic sway which so many mothers-in-law are but too well disposed to exercise over their daughters-in-law.

The Rev. Gentleman alludes again and again in his letter to the state of contempt and degradation in which, in his opinion, the Hindoo fair sex in India is held.

I have already observed, that that apparent contempt was nothing but a matter of form, and merely ceremonial; and I will now add, that in no country are women in reality more respected in public than in India.

In fact, among the Hindoos the person of a woman is sacred. She cannot be touched in public by a man, even with the end of the fingers. How abject soever may be her condition, she is never addressed by any body, not excepting the persons of the highest rank, but under the respectful name of *mother* (umma). A dwelling in which only females are to be found, even the hut of the most helpless widow, is an inviolable asylum into which the most determined libertine would never dare to penetrate; or, should he do it, his audacity would not remain unpunished. A woman can frequent the most crowded places without being exposed to the least insult. A male who would stop merely to gaze on a female who is passing by, as our loungers in Europe are accustomed to do, would be considered by all as an insolent and uneducated person. Even a mere look designed to insult a woman would be resented and avenged. In short, the least insult by words or otherwise, the least mark of disrespect offered in public to a female, is instantly resented and avenged by her husband, her sons, or her brothers, who would expose themselves to all dangers rather than overlook an offence offered to their wives, their mothers, or sisters, or see them treated in public with disregard.

"What mothers! (exclaims the Rev. ——) without a knowledge of the alphabet, and unacquainted with all the employments of females in a civilized country."

To be sure, they will not dance *waltzes*, or deliver in any other way their persons into the arms of another man. They are too well aware of what they owe to their husbands, and to the modesty of their sex, to allow themselves such gross violations of decorum; but what I have already stated, and what I am still about to state, will prove that although "without a knowledge of the alphabet," they are dutiful daughters, faithful wives, tender mothers, and intelligent housewives; and they are not in fact, as shamelessly asserted by the Rev. Gentleman, "mere animals kept for slaughter or for burden in the houses of their husbands."

In fact, there is perhaps no kind of honest employment in a civilized country in which the Hindoo females have not a due share. Besides the management of the household, and the care of the family, which are (as already noticed) under their controul, the wives and daughters of husbandmen attend, and assist their husbands and fathers in the labours of agriculture. Those of tradesmen assist theirs in carrying on their trade. Merchants are attended and assisted by theirs in their shops. Many females are shopkeepers on their own account; and *without a knowledge of the alphabet*, or of the decimal scale, they keep by other means their accounts in excellent order, and are considered as still shrewder than the males themselves in their commercial dealings. Several shops entirely kept by females, without the help of males, may be seen in large towns in every bazar street. I have sometimes observed female shopkeepers sitting down cross-legged in their shops, and serving their customers with the greatest ease and affability. A greater number are seen selling fish, betel, flowers, vegetables, fruits, and sundry articles of subsistence or furniture. The poor classes, which unfortunately form the majority of the population, let themselves as servants or journey-women, or earn otherwise a scanty subsistence by selling grass, fuel, straw, &c. &c. In short, there is no kind of work, no kind of trade, in a civilized society, in which the Hindoo females are not seen actively engaged, and occupying a conspicuous place. I am acquainted with industrious widows, who, having undertaken a small trade with a trifling capital of forty or fifty rupees, have, by their economy, their labours, and industry, increased it, within these past ten years, to the amount of five or six hundred.

Such are, however, the individuals, whom the Reverend ——, is pleased to represent, as "spending their lives in inanity and idleness, and as mere animals kept for slaughter or for burden in the houses of their husbands."

I am happy that a long experience has taught me on the subject a theory quite different from his, and to view the Hindoo fair sex in a much more favourable light. At the same time, I believe that it may be said without giving offence, that the Europeans are not qualified to form a fair judgment on the subject, on account of the difficulty, not to say impossibility, of holding a free and confidential intercourse with the respectable part of the Hindoo females. All their knowledge in this respect is derived from their criminal connections with concubines, ordinarily of the lowest tribes, or other females of the most dissolute dispositions. Hence arise the false notions of the Europeans. The knowledge I have attained on the subject is not hearsay, but from personal observations. My profession has afforded me repeated opportunities to become acquainted with the character of the Hindoo females, and by living with them on a footing of paternal familiarity I have had numberless opportunities of conversing with them without restraint. Their conversation on subjects connected with their internal economy and domestic concerns was not certainly destitute of interest, and on all other subjects within their reach I have generally found them communicative, gay, and lively.

I do not mean that they are free from the defects of their sex. They are, in common with the females of all countries, exceedingly fond of jewels and *parure*, covetous, obstinate, irascible, vindictive, capricious, fickle, talkative to excess, slanderous, and in too many instances quarrelsome.

In another of his productions, the Reverend —— had, by a sweeping phrase, indiscriminately branded the Hindoo fair sex with lewdness, by insinuating that "a chaste female was almost unknown among the Hindoos." I can confidently affirm that this shameful accusation is unfounded. Knowing that the same unjust suspicions respecting the virtue of the Hindoo fair were entertained by many prejudiced and misinformed Europeans, I have made diligent enquiries to know how far such an injurious slander was grounded on fact; and as my profession has enabled me to live on a certain footing of familiary with the persons of both sexes, and to entertain with them a confidential intercourse, I think that my information may be depended upon. I have generally observed that amongst *good castes*, the Hindoo females in general, and married women in particular, were worthy to be set forth as patterns of chastity, and conjugal fidelity, to the persons of their sex in more enlightened countries. I do not mean that breaches of those virtues never occur amongst the former; but I believe that they happen still more seldom with them than with the persons of their sex in countries which boast to have reached a much higher degree of civilization.

Such is the result of my own observations; and I am confident that every unprejudiced person, who will attend to the subject with the same impartiality, and disinterestedness, as myself, will render the same homage to the virtue of the Hindoo fair sex.

The Reverend —— finds fault also with the Hindoo females, because they are unacquainted with needle-work: "they are unable (says he) either to make, to mend, or to wash the clothes of their households." He might have added, "and to make or mend their shoes."

Is the reverend gentleman ignorant, that there are every where in India, as well as in Europe, tailors, washermen, and shoemakers. That these professions, as well as every other, are exercised by castes, to which they belong exclusively, and that the individuals who compose those castes, both males and females, are obliged for a trifling salary to discharge the duties of their profession whenever called upon for the purpose by the other tribes? Is he ignorant that the clothes of the females, and those of the great majority of the males, are composed of a single piece without seams, and that needle-work and tailors were of course unknown and useless to them, until comparatively of late years, when the Mahometan dress was partly adopted by small numbers of them, among the persons in office.

But instead of needle-work, which can be of no utility to them, the Hindoo females are almost all acquainted with the art of spinning cotton, and immense numbers get a livelihood by this means. There are few houses in which reels are not to be found, and after having finished their other domestic businesses, instead of spending their leisure "in inanity and idleness," as the Reverend —— says, or of passing their time at a card-table, as do most European ladies, they are seen sitting down cross-legged on a mat, and spinning cotton for sale, or for manufacturing the coarse clothes with which they cover themselves, accompanying these simple and useful occupations with some decent song, or playing and prattling with their children. Since hosiery has become an object of trade, they are acquainted with the mode of knitting stockings, and numbers are at present seen earning a livelihood in this way.

The Rev. —— says, in rather bad humour, that " the Hindoo females are obliged to go veiled, when they leave their houses, and that they never mix in public companies."

These statements are quite incorrect. The Hindoo females were at no period veiled; they always were, and are still seen, both at home and abroad, with their heads, or at least their faces, uncovered. In some provinces they make their appearance in public, with their bodies immodestly exposed, from their heads to their middles; and every where, the Brahmin females in particular, uncover not only their whole heads, but also the hind parts of their legs to their hams, and sometimes higher, in a manner which, to the eyes of an European, appears very indecent.

It is untrue, also, that the women in India are excluded from all public assemblies. So far from this being the case, it is very well known that it is they who are the leaders, and act the principal part in the most solemn family ceremonies, such as those of wedding, of the *cord*, &c. &c., while the males remain, as it were, passive spectators in those crowded assemblies. It is also well known, that it is they who are the leaders in all the numerous religious feasts celebrated by the Hindoos, in their houses, during the course of the year, such as those of *oogohdy*, the pongol, mahunavamy, &c. &c.

On the other hand, if the reverend gentleman had witnessed any one of those solemn processions performed by the Hindoos, in the streets, he would have remarked that the females, in several instances, composed the majority of the crowd that attended them. If he had had a sight of the places of worship, during the celebration of the mysteries of the religion of the country, he would have observed that they were attended by a number of females, nearly equal to that of the males. If he had been present in the market-streets when any farce or other public spectacle is exhibited by quacks, jugglers, and other mountebanks, he would have seen that in several instances the women formed the majority amongst the spectators. In a word, with a little more attention to the subject, and a little less prejudice, he would have observed that the Hindoo females were to be met with every where, and had their full share in most public assemblies, both religious and profane; and would have paused before he uttered these reprehensible words, that they were in fact mere *animals*, kept "for slaughter, or for burden, in the houses of their husbands."

The Rev. —— returns again to the stale subject of the burning of the Hindoo widows, on the pile of their deceased husbands, and quotes the lamentable fact of seven hundred and six victims having devoted themselves to that barbarous superstition, in the course of the year 1817, in the presidency of Bengal. It is a well-known fact, (as I observed in a former letter,) that these nefarious sacrifices have increased of late years; but the reverend gentleman is not perhaps apprized, that many persons of good sense, who have made enquiries about the causes of this increasing evil, have been of opinion, that its aggravation was in a great measure owing to his intemperate zeal, and that of many of his associates in the work of reform. He is not, perhaps, aware, that owing to their abrupt attacks on the most deep-laid prejudices of the country, the zeal of the Hindoos had been roused to a determined spirit of opposition and resistance, when they saw their most sacred customs and practices publicly reviled, laughed at, and turned into ridicule, by words, and in writing, in numberless religious tracts, circulated with profusion, in every direction, all over the country.

Those horrid suicides, called *Suttees*, have unfortunately prevailed from the earliest times to the present in the country, chiefly in the north of India, and the putting a stop to them altogether, by coercion, appears a measure too pregnant with danger to be attempted. In the moral order, as well as the physical, we are often reduced to the sad necessity of tolerating great evils not to be exposed to greater ones.

Those execrable sacrifices occur but seldom in the south of the Peninsula. I suppose that the population of the country on this side of the Krishna, does not fall short of thirty millions, and I am persuaded, that the number of *suttees* does not amount to thirty in a year. But thirty suttees in a year, in a population of thirty millions, are certainly by far too many; and nobody deplores, more bitterly than I do, those horrid excesses of superstition and fanaticism.

But, after all, is suicide confined to the Hindoo widows; and are our countries free from such detestable excesses? So far from this being the case, I am persuaded that more persons perish in France and England, in a month, through suicide and duelling, than during a whole year in India, through *suttees*. The only difference I can remark, between the one and the other, is, that the deluded Hindoo widow commits suicide from misled religious motives, and from what she considers as an indispensable duty of conjugal devotion; whilst the European suicide puts an end to his existence, in defiance of every religious restraint, and in open violation of his most sacred duties towards God, and towards men.

Shall, therefore, our whole compassion be engrossed by the Hindoo widow, and shall we not reserve a tear, or a sigh, for our still more guilty and more unfortunate countrymen?

Are suicide and duelling in Europe less nefarious than suttees in India? Why, then, is the deluded Hindoo widow arraigned with so much severity, while the laws against duellists are dormant, and the tribunals of justice generally under the necessity of overlooking those deliberate and malicious murderers?

The Rev. ——, in order to render the Hindoo females more and more abject and despicable, quotes two or three shocking stories, which, if they are not altogether false, are at least misrepresented and exaggerated to such a degree as to render his accounts entirely unworthy of credit. He says, for instance, that "parents, in some cases, marry fifty or sixty daughters to a single Brahmin." I question whether a single case of such turpitude might be cited among the thirty millions of inhabitants, who people this side of the Peninsula; and I am persuaded, that if such instances occur in Bengal, they are rare, and that the few Brahmins who may allow themselves such open transgression of the usages of their caste, are spurned and shunned by the individuals of their tribe who preserve any sense of honour; for polygamy is strongly discouraged by the Hindoo customs among all castes, and above all, in that of the Brahmins, among whom marriage is generally confined to the pair.

"Every mother (exclaims the reverend gentleman) among the tribe of Rajahpoots puts her female child to death as soon as born."

This odious paragraph is one of the most shocking slanders contained in the author's letter. There is a good proportion of married Rajahpoot sepoys in every battalion of the native army. I appeal to all the British officers of each battalion, serving under the three presidencies, and I boldly defy them to quote a single instance of this horrid kind.

There are, in every province of the Peninsula, numbers of Rajahpoot families. I have been acquainted with many individuals of this high-minded tribe, and I am quite sure that there is no one who would not shudder at such an execrable imputation.

I have, indeed, been informed, that this detestable practice formerly prevailed to a certain degree in some districts in the north of India, among two or three subdivisions of Rajahpoots, for this tribe, as well as every other, is subdivided at least into twenty others; but the Reverend —— cannot be ignorant that owing to the mild, humane, and insinuative exertions of the late Governor Duncan, (a circumstance which will shed an unperishable lustre over the memory of that excellent man,) a stop was put to those abominable murders.

On this subject, the Reverend —— adds the following horrid story: "While in Bengal (says he) *I was informed* of the case of a Rajahpoot taking his daughter aside, and with a hatchet cutting her to pieces."

I am firmly persuaded that the informer of the Reverend —— imposed a downright falsehood on his credulity, or, if the fact proves authentic, it originated in causes quite different from those alleged by that author.

Among the domestic regulations peculiar to the tribe of the Rajahpoots, one of the most remarkable is that by which adultery (as was the case under the Mosaical law) is punished with death; and I have no doubt, that if the story related to the Reverend —— is authentic, the slaughter of that female by her own father originated in her having dishonoured both herself and family, by giving herself up to foreign loves.

It appears that the Reverend —— has chiefly derived his knowledge of the Hindoos from informers, and to this source, above all, I am willing to attribute the many inaccuracies, exaggerations, and misrepresentations which abound in his writings. That writer should have been aware that the Hindoo informers in general, before giving information on any subject, begin by studying the character and temper, the dispositions and bias of their employers, and to give them information accordingly. Those employed by the reverend gentleman, seeing him disposed to blacken and debase the Hindoos by all means, and in all manners, served him according to his taste.

I never employed informers in my researches and enquiries about the Hindoos, my scanty means not allowing me to keep persons of this description in my service. What I have written on the subject is the result of my personal observations, in an unrestrained intercourse with people of all castes and religions, during a period of thirty years almost entirely passed among the natives; and on the subject of this article, I can confidently assure you that the Hindoo parents of all castes, above all, mothers, if equalled by any people on the earth in tenderness towards their progeny, both males and females, are surely surpassed by none; nay, it might be said, that their parental tenderness is rather carried to excess, and owing to that excessive fondness, their children of both sexes are spoiled and rendered vicious.

I have reserved the review of the most audacious paragraph of the author's address for the end of this letter: it is that where he emphatically exclaims, "What must be the state of the female mind, when *millions* are found throwing the children of their vows into the sea?" &c. &c.

I will confess that I could not refrain from shuddering at the perusal of this atrocious paragraph, and I am surprized that the public authorities at home have taken no notice of such a slander; the tendency of which is to cast an indelible stain of infamy on the country government. Good God! "Millions of females throwing the children of their vows into the sea;" and doing so in the face of day, under the eyes of a government famed all over the earth for its spirit of humanity, of justice, and benevolence! Of what exotic materials must not be composed the mind of that Englishman, when he dares bring forward falsehoods which tend to nothing less than to cast eternal disgrace on his nation, and his countrymen; for, if it were true that "millions of mothers are found throwing the children of their vows into the sea," and the government should remain passive and indifferent spectator of so many horrid murders, such a government would deserve to be held forth to the execration of all Europe, and of all the civilized world, and its memory handed down with everlasting infamy to the remotest posterity.

I will observe here, that a superstition prevails all over the country derived from astrological notions, according to which when children are born under certain stars which are supposed to possess a particularly malignant influence, they are in a very few cases secretly put to death, or thrown into a river; but such instances of horror are fortunately rare, the children born in such inauspicious circumstances being ordinarly exposed on the high roads, and when found out, are taken by some compassionate person, educated, and fostered by him with nearly as much care as his own progeny.

The Reverend —— ought to have stated the fact such as it is, and he ought, moreover, in justice to truth, to have added that the Bengal government (under the presidency of the Marquis Wellesley, I believe,) had no sooner been made acquainted with the existence of this horrid practice than resolutions were passed, by which it was declared that the persons who were guilty of those execrable excesses should, when discovered, be put upon their trials as guilty of wilful murder, and judged according to the severity of the laws. But the reverend gentleman has very uncandidly, and very unmanly, overlooked all these circumstances, as he was determined to represent these poor Hindoos under the blackest and most odious colours.

That author finishes his address to the ladies of Liverpool by a kind of Don-Quixote appeal to their sensibility, and compassion, for the purpose of soliciting their support and assistance towards the establishment of schools to enlighten the Hindoo females.

The ladies of Liverpool are not aware, I suppose, that such a project is merely visionary, and altogether impracticable, the most deeply rooted prejudices of the country being decidedly hostile to its execution.

The ladies of Liverpool are not aware, that even should not the prejudices of the country oppose an almost insurmountable bar to the establishment of schools for females in India, the state of poverty of the latter, and their numerous avocations, would not allow them to attend those schools.

The ladies of Liverpool are not aware, that at least five-sixths of the Hindoo females live in such distressed circumstances, that from the age of eight or ten years, to the end of their lives, they are obliged to labour without intermission from morning till evening, and that, notwithstanding their uncessant labours, they are hardly capable of saving enough to purchase a coarse cloth of the value of five or six shillings, to cover themselves.

If I were to make an appeal to the charity and compassion of the ladies of Liverpool, or of any other town in the United Kingdom, I would advise them to look around themselves, and behold the distressing spectacle of misery which most unfortunately prevails to such an alarming extent among the lower classes of their own countrymen, and represent to them, as an imperative duty, the obligation of employing all their savings to assist their neighbours, and alleviate by all the means in their power the evils of the distressed persons who live around them. In doing so, I should only enforce the duties of that holy religion which imperatively commands the rich to share his substance with the poor; the affluent to assist the needy. Or if those ladies were disposed to give a more extensive range to their charity and benevolence, and to cause the distressed among the Hindoos to share their liberality, I would advise them to intrust, to the hands of some friend in India, the sums destined for the purpose, recommending him to make a proper selection among the numberless naked, emaciated, and starving individuals of both sexes who are to be found in every place in the country, and to distribute the sums amongst those who were most worthy of compassion.

But I shall certainly never call on any lady, or other individual whatever, to engage him or her to squander away the money in contributing to the (in my humble opinion) absurd project of establishing schools for the purpose of enlightening the Hindoo females, or of circulating Bibles and tracts which are perused by no one, and are above the comprehension of all.

I remain, &c.

1*st October*, 1821.

## To J. S. Esq.

My dear Sir,

In my last I informed you, that I would take the first moments of leisure I could spare, to give you my opinion on the printed *Canada* translation, of the first four chapters of the book of *Genesis*, which you did me the honor to submit to my criticism. I have thought that the best way of performing this task, was to send you a literal translation into English from the Canada version, in order that you may be able to judge of the merits of the latter yourself; you will see from the accompanying translated chapter, that there is scarcely a single verse in that version, which may be said to have been accurately translated, and that in several instances the meaning of the text is perverted or materially changed.

If you entertain suspicions as to the genuineness of my translation, as there are I suppose, Brahmin writers in your office, acquainted with both languages, you can show them both the Canada version, and my English translation, and I trust that they will do justice to the correctness of the latter.

The other chapters are equally incorrect, both as to the meaning and the style. The latter has appeared so low, and so ludicrous, to several natives of good sense, whom I desired to peruse the whole attentively, that they all expressed themselves with marks of contempt and disgust at such a performance; and they all agreed in saying, that if it were intended to render the Christian religion for ever contemptible and odious to the pagan Hindoos, there were no surer means to attain this end, than to exhibit to them our sacred records under such a despicable garb.

I have been so thoroughly disgusted in going through the translation of the first chapter, that I beg you will excuse me the trouble of translating the three others. For I cannot disguise to you, that as a most sincere believer in the divine origin of our Holy Scriptures, I cannot help experiencing the most distressing feelings of indignation, when I see those sublime books, the sacred word of God himself, so basely, so shamefully, so sacrilegiously defaced, debased, and perverted, and held out under such a shape to the very enemies of our holy religion, as the pure word of God.

If one of the many proofs of our holy books being of divine origin be derived from their intrinsical worth, from their noble, inimitable, and majestic simplicity, there is, alas! on the other hand, but too much reason to fear that the Hindoos will form a directly opposite judgment on the subject, when they behold the ludicrous, vulgar, and almost unintelligible style of the versions at present circulated among them; and that even the most reasonable and best disposed, in beholding our Holy Scriptures under such a contemptible shape, so far from looking upon them as the word of God, will on the contrary be strongly impelled to consider them as forgeries of some obscure, ignorant, and illiterate individual, and of course a downright imposture.

It is, however, to execute such performances, (for the Tamoul and Telinga versions, parts of which I have also perused, have not appeared to me superior to this,) that public credulity in Europe is imposed upon, and immense sums of money are subscribed.

You may rest persuaded, that all those *soi-disant* translations will soon find their way to the bazar streets, to be sold there, as waste paper, to the country grocers, for the purpose of wrapping their drugs in them; and indeed, in my humble opinion, they are fit for nothing else.

I express to you my sentiments on the subject with candour, and without hypocrisy, as you have requested me so to do, and I am ready fearlessly to express the same, in the presence of the Bible Society itself, and of all the universities in Europe; for my opinion, (let them give it the appellation of prejudice, of ignorance, or obstinacy, it is the same to me,) being grounded on an inward conviction, the result of a long and attentive experience, is unalterable.

I remain &c. &c.

11*th June*, 1821.

## *A literal Translation of the Canada Version of the first Chapter of the Book of Genesis.*

### ACCOUNT OF MOSES.

### CHAPTER I.

1. In the beginning God created the earth and the air. (*a*)

2. But the earth was *uneven* and empty, and there was darkness *over water*; but God's *soul* (*b*) *was roaming with delight* (*c*) on water.

(*a*) Air is the literal meaning of the word *accossa*, and conveys to the mind a quite different idea from that of the heaven (cœlum) of Scripture, which ought to be translated by the word *para-loca*.

(*b*) This expression, *Dewer-attma*, literally, God's soul, is different from the *spirit* (spiritus) of Scripture, and must convey to a man unacquainted with the scriptural style, the idea of a corporeal being, composed of a soul and a body.

(*c*) Such is the literal meaning of the compound verb *lol-ahdvovadoo*, to roam or wander with delight (as a spirited horse would when let loose).

3. Next God said, Let *brightness* (*d*) be made! Then brightness was made.

4. God seeing that *brightness* was good, he separated *brightness* from *obscurity*. (*e*)

5. God gave to *brightness* the name of day, and to *obscurity* the name of night; and *whereas in this manner the evening and the morning came to pass,* it was the first day.

6. Next God said, Let the *orb of space* (*f*) be made in the midst of water, and let it be separated *from this water, and from that water.* (*g*)

7. *In this very manner* God having created *the orb of space*, He divided the water which was above *the orb of space*, and the water which was below *the orb of space*, and it was made so.

8. He gave the name of *air* to the *orb of space*; and *whereas in this manner* the evening

(*d*) The literal meaning of the word *bilakoo* is *brightness*, in French *clarté*, different from the *light* (lux) of Scripture, which should be translated by the word *pracassa*.

(*e*) *Kattlai* literally means *obscurity*, and differs from the *darkness* (tenebræ) of Scripture, which ought to be translated by the word *antacara*.

(*f*) Such is the meaning of the words *vissala-mandala*, different from the *firmament* of Scripture, which ought to be translated by the word *gagana*.

(*g*) The meaning of the text is entirely changed in this phrase.

and the morning *came to pass*, it was the second day.

9. *Next* God said, Let the water that is under the *air* collect together in one place, and let the dry earth be seen! and it was made so.

10. God gave to the dry land the name of earth, and to the waters collected together the name of sea, and God saw that it was good.

11. Then God said, Let the earth germinate herbs and plants giving seeds; *and besides that*, let seeds being made, they make germinate according to their species, trees giving fruits! and it was made so. (*h*)

12. Then the earth made germinate herbs, and plants giving seeds according to their species; *and besides that*, trees having seeds and giving fruits according to their species; and God saw that it was good.

13. *And whereas in this manner* the evening and morning *came to pass*, it was the third day.

14. *But* God said, Let there be in *the orb of space, that is air*, light, to divide the day from the night, and let them be *to make*

(*h*) It is not the exact meaning of the text.

*known* the signs, and times, and nights and days.

15. And let them be lights *in the orb of space, that is air,* for the purpose of shining on the earth, and it was made so.

16. God created two great lights: one great light *to govern* the day, and a smaller light *to govern* the night and the stars.

17. And God placed them *in the orb of space, that is air,* in order to shine on the earth, and *to govern* the day and night, and to separate *obscurity* from *brightness;* and God saw that it was good.

18. And *whereas in this manner* the evening and the morning *came to pass,* it was the fourth day.

19. Next God said, Let there be made in the water *a great many moving aquatic insects,* and the birds which are on the earth and fly *in the orb of space, that is air!*

20. *In this manner* God created a great many *large fishes* which were born in the water, each one according to its own species, and the *moving aquatic insects,* and the several species of winged *tribes,* and the birds of all kinds; and God saw that it was good.

21. Then God blessed them, saying, fishes increase and multiply, *and be in great numbers*

in the water of sea! *all birds* multiply on the earth. (*i*)

22. *And whereas in this manner* the evening and morning *came* to pass, it was the fifth day.

23. Next God said, Let the earth give birth to the several species of living creatures, of cows (*k*), of *moving insects,* and to all the tribes of the beasts of forests; and it was made so.

24. In this manner God created the several tribes of beasts on the earth; the several tribes of horned cattle (*l*), and the several tribes of *insects* moving on the earth: and he saw that it was good.

25. Next God said, Let us create a man *similar to us, and having our form!* Let him command the *aquatic insects* of the sea; the birds that fly in the air; the beasts having life; all earth; and *the insects* that move on the earth.

26. In this manner God created a man *having his form.* He created him *having the*

(*i*) The *italic* words, in this verse, are mere interpolations not to be found in the text.

(*k*) The word *passoovoo,* when alone, means *cows.* It means animals in general only when the word *pranei* (passoovoo pranei) is added to it.

(*l*) These words are an interpolation not to be found in the text.

*figure of God.* (*m*) Moreover, he created him male and female.

27. Then God blessing them, said, Increase and multiply, and filling the earth, *overcome it;* and command the fishes of the sea, and the birds of the air, and all the animals that move on the earth.

28. *Moreover* God said, Lo! I have given you all the species of plants producing seeds, with which *all the earth is filled*, and all species of trees, *nay, trees* producing fruits, and having seeds, they shall be a food for you.

29. And he said, I have given the herbs and plants as a food for all the animals on the earth which have life, and for all the birds that fly in the air, and for all the insects that move on the earth; and it was made so.

30. Then God saw all that he had created, and it was *perfect;* and *whereas in this manner* the evening and the morning *came to pass*, it was the sixth day. (*n*)

(*m*) Blasphemous expressions.

(*n*) *Ex uno disce omnes.* The other chapters are equally incorrect, and abundant in errors. Besides that, the style is quite ludicrous; and there is no Hindoo scholar who can keep a serious countenance in perusing such a performance.

*N.B.* The words in *italics* are those whose meaning materially differs from that of the text.

To Captain M. C.

My dear Sir,

I return you, with my thanks, the two accompanying curious books *, which I have perused with interest, inasmuch as they clearly make it out, that in this supposed highly refined and improved age, fraud and roguery have taken hold of most professions and trades; and quackery or imposture of most religions and beliefs. The one lays open the impositions practised on the body, and the other those practised on the soul. In perusing the latter, I have been stricken by the similarity I have remarked between the leading tenets of several Christian sects described therein, and those prevailing among the pagan Hindoos. It is a common custom among you Protestants, to upbraid us Catholics with idolatry, on account of our images, processions, holy water, fasts, &c. But I find from Mr. Evans's Sketch, that we could retort on yourselves your arguments on the subject

* Accum on Culinary Poisons, and Evans's Sketch of the Christian Sects.

with great advantage. In fact, in many of your leading tenets and practices, you cannot even claim the merits of originality, since it may be said that you have had the idolatrous Hindoos for leaders and teachers. I find, for instance, that the leading dogmas of the Predestinarians, Necessitarians, Antinomians, and others, have, from time immemorial, been fully upheld and professed by the Hindoos, in the sects or schools known under the name of *Vedantans* and *Mimansam*, of which I have given a short sketch in the new edition of my former work.

On the other hand, I can perceive between the religious exercises of the Quakers, Methodists, Jumpers, Shakers, &c. &c., and those of the Hindoo Dassaroo, Jangoomas, Andys, &c., no difference, unless that the religious practices of the former, surpass by far in in folly and extravagance those of the latter. Both, in their convulsions and contortions, in their wild dancing, jumping, groaning, howling, own a common origin, that is, the inspiration or possession of a supernatural spirit or agent. The only difference is (as I have just remarked) that our European *Energumenes* leave their Hindoo brethren far behind them in the career of extravagance.

But the article which has stricken me most

in that little work, is that of the *Millennium*, which is nothing but an almost literal copy of the tenth *Avattera* of Vishnoo, called Kalky-avattera, or incarnation into a horse.* This Avattera, of which I give a description in my new edition, is to put an end to the corruption, fraud, and injustice introduced among men by the last *Bouhda-avattera*, and cause virtue, lasting peace, and complete happiness to reign on earth among the human race. Such is exactly to be the effect produced, at the very same period, during the age of the *millennarians*, and when the latter contrived their *millennium*, I cannot refrain from believing that they had a knowledge of the *kalky-avattara*. Both systems coincide so perfectly in their origin, motives, and effects, that the one must have been copied out from the other.

If it were justifiable to jest upon a subject which has at all times filled me with awe, or to slight a religion which I most sincerely and most firmly believe to be the only true one upon earth, I could carry on this disgusting parallel to a much fuller extent; but I will conclude it, as the subject is too serious

* Which is to take place to the end of the Cahly yoogam.

to become a matter of raillery. The only thing that vexes me is the strong hold that all those opposite and jarring interpretations of the unerring word of the God of all truth cannot fail to give unbelievers and other enemies to Christianity.

I remain, &c.

*22d November*, 1821.

THE END.